WILD SOUNDSCAPES

Dedication

For Kat

WILD SOUNDSCAPES

Discovering the Voice of the Natural World

A Book and CD Recording

BERNIE KRAUSE

WILDERNESS PRESS
BERKELEY

FIRST EDITION May 2002

All photographs by the author except where otherwise noted.
Back cover author photo copyright © 2002 Fred Mertz

Book and CD design: Larry B. Van Dyke
Editor: Jannie Dresser
Visionary Publisher: Mike Jones
Cakes and ale: Katherine Krause

Animal imagery reprinted courtesy of Dover Publications,
Animals: 1419 Copyright-Free Illustrations

Library of Congress Card Catalog Number 2002066168
International Standard Book Number 0-89997-296-9
UPC 7-19609-97296-9

Manufactured in the United States of America

Published by **Wilderness Press**
　　　　　　1200 5th Street
　　　　　　Berkeley, CA 94710
　　　　　　(800) 443-7227
　　　　　　Fax (510) 558-1696
　　　　　　mail@wildernesspress.com
　　　　　　www.wildernesspress.com

Visit our website for a complete listing of Wilderness Press books and maps

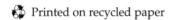 Printed on recycled paper

Library of Congress Cataloging-in-Publication Data

Krause, Bernard L.
    Wild soundscapes : discovering the voice of the natural world : a book and CD
recording / Bernie Krause. — 1st ed.
        p. cm.
    Includes bibliographical references (p.).
    ISBN 0-89997-296-9
    1. Nature sounds—Recording and reproducing. I. Title.
QH510.5 .K735 2002
508'.028'4—dc21

　　　　　　　　　　　　　　　　　　　　　　　　　2002066168

Preface

Over a year and a half ago, I approached Wilderness Press with a book on listening to and recording natural sound. I've been a sound recording professional for over 40 years, and a bioacoustician specializing in the sounds of nature since 1968. Although natural sound recording is something of a specialized field, I had arrived at the conclusion that many techniques and pieces of equipment had become accessible to anyone with the time and interest, as well as an inclination to make a small investment in some basic sound equipment. It was my feeling that the special pleasure of being outdoors and recording wild sounds was and should be experienced by as many people as possible, in much the same way that many have enhanced and recorded their outdoor adventures by taking snapshots, filming, or videotaping what they see.

The ability to hear and interpret what we hear is primal. Like most creatures in the animal kingdom, our species has depended on hearing as a key to survival. Our awareness of sounds and the structure of our brains developed in an organic dance within the environments we occupied. We live in a much different world than our prehistoric ancestors, however, and as I will show in this book, our sense of hearing took a back seat as we relied more and more on our sense of sight to discover and interpret our world. Our current mechanized environments, with their noise and clatter, have distanced us even further from the pleasure we take in our sense of hearing. Many are losing *sensitivity* to the voices of the natural wild that are both supportive and healing. And, an alarming number of us are losing all or part of our ability to hear due to the increasing volume and intrusiveness of human-manufactured noise. Yet, we have hardly begun to study the impact of noise on our nervous systems, let alone its damage to the natural world.

The publication of *Wild Soundscapes* coincides with a decision by the United States National Park Service to develop an education program to teach the public about natural sounds and their relationship to creature habitats. As vital as our old-growth forests, wilderness areas, and endangered species are, the wild soundscapes of our public and privately-held lands are essential national treasures that are increasingly vulnerable to human impact. Overpopulation, easy accessibility, the excavation and use of minerals and fossil fuels, and, in particular, a mentality that sees nature and wilderness as resources to exploit and "manage," have led to serious consequences for many of our native forests, deserts, plains, woodlands and waterways from sea to shining sea. Any disturbed natural zone is disturbed in full: the water, air, soil, plants, and animals are all affected. Sound, whether the vocalization of a particular creature or the thundering roar of a snowmobile, helicopter, dirt bike, or jet ski, physically changes any setting in which it is heard or felt in ways we do not completely understand. This is something people living closer to the wild natural, who are totally engaged within their physical surroundings, better understand.

I wrote this book to share my love of the natural world and its voice, as well as to contribute to efforts to improve our relationship with the wild. Awareness of natural sound can educate us about natural forces and creature habitats, and lead to efforts to protect the environment. The wild natural is to enjoy and treasure, to defend in a responsible and respectful manner. I am delighted the National Park Service has come to regard sound as part of the equation, and hope its action augurs well, so that legislators, policy-makers, property owners, and the public will follow suit.

At the back of the book is a compact disc to give you some examples of wild soundscapes you can discover, as well as some techniques you might want to acquire. Wilderness Press is ordinarily a publisher of outdoor recreational guidebooks. This book doesn't tell you where the trails are, or how rough or easy, or how long. This book is not only a how-to, but a where-to, what-to, and why-to. I hope it answers many questions about natural sound even as it raises questions that you can answer when you listen carefully to your own wild soundscapes.

I am most grateful to the collective human voices, now silent, whose spiritual and intellectual guidance have brought joy and exhilaration to my life. The most resonant were John Muir, Aldo Leopold, Rachel Carson, Ralph Waldo Emerson, Edward Abbey, and Walt Whitman, among others. Of those still heard, I am profoundly indebted to Lang Elliott, Stuart Gage, Wes Henry, Keri Hulme, W.A. Mathieu, Roger Payne, Louis Sarno, R. Murray Schafer, Bill Schmidt, Florence Shepard, Rudy Trubitt, and the visionary writings of many other contemporaries too numerous to mention. The manuscript that has emerged from chaos and polemic to what I hope is a helpful and informative declaration of the world of natural sound is a result of the insight, wit, intelligence, and diligence that constantly springs from Jannie Dresser, my ever-patient editor at Wilderness Press. Mike Jones, the publisher, shined through with an abundance of faith in a different kind of project. Larry Van Dyke worked hard to create a beautifully designed book. And, thanks to the other staff at Wilderness Press who contributed to the improved text.

None of the life that I have enjoyed and the few words that I have found to describe it would have been remotely possible without my partner, my wife, my lover, and most honest critic, Katherine. E.M. Forster once defined love as tolerance, sympathy, and good humor. Kat has taken these virtues to new levels of expression that even Forester would have envied. She has endured hardship with me on field trips and at home, suffered through many drafts and revisions of the manuscript, and has kept me honest to a fault and I love her dearly.

—Bernie Krause
Glen Ellen, California
May 2002

Contents

Foreword

by Roger Payne

I have always preferred radio to television, agreeing with the old saw that in radio "the images are better." Back in the 1970s I encountered a wonderful example of that. One summer's night I found myself out late in Algonquin Park in Canada. We were howling for wolves—trying to record them. Although we got a single very faint answer from a distant wolf, it was not what we wanted; the rest of the recordings from that evening were just the local ambient natural sounds, including the trickle of a nearby brook, some crickets, and a distant wood thrush that was up later than usual, singing its final evening vespers.

During a hard snowstorm in the following winter, I was searching through some tapes for whale songs when I happened upon a tape that was marked with a note saying it had nothing on it and was reusable. I couldn't imagine what it was, so I put it on. There was the distant wood thrush in his acoustic surrounding: its recorded song instantly transported me back to that summer evening in Canada. The sounds created a flood of feeling, lifting me out of my winter surroundings and setting me down in the midst of hot summer. I can even remember feeling warm, for a moment. This was accomplished more strongly than I would have imagined possible, even though the outside world was frozen clean through its heart. It was a powerful lesson, demonstrating to me that sounds are more evocative than any other sense, even more evocative than the sense of smell where subtle whiffs of familiar odors—such as the smell of grandmother's house—are able to bring back vivid memories from past decades.

Bernie Krause apparently feels the same way. He notes in this interesting and useful book that: "When recorded sound is at its best, nothing in the human-created visual world, by itself, even comes close to its impact." He tells the story of when he recorded a jaguar that had followed him through the Amazon jungle one night; after he set up his recording gear and moved a few feet off, the jaguar came silently up to his microphone, sniffed it and than made a low growl. As Krause points out, a photograph of such an event might cause you to smile nervously, but listening to the recording of the jaguar sniffing and growling, makes the hair on the back of your neck stand up. Krause includes the recording on the compact disc that accompanies this book; you are unlikely ever to forget it—it is utterly chilling. When you listen to it, ask yourself if any moving image has ever evoked such an intense response in you.

Because of the evocative nature of sound, Krause regrets that so few people have either the equipment or the knowledge to record the sounds that would, when listened to later, transport them back to places and situations they have loved, and do better than pictures ever can. One of the most useful parts of his book describes how to get equipped at reasonable cost. He recommends specific pieces of equipment and explains what microphones to use and how they will affect the final result. He also describes some of the tricks of the recording trade.

The most important point made in *Wild Soundscapes* is that it is not the single, dissected-out, cleanly recorded voices of nature that transport you back most vividly to the places where, and the times when, you recorded them. The best 'beaming up' occurs only when such voices are embedded in their own acoustic surroundings—what Krause refers to as their biophonies and geophonies (*biophonies* being the voices of living things, and *geophonies* being the non-creature sounds of the earth such as thunder, rain, and wind).

Biologists such as Krause and myself focus on recording natural soundscapes to secure the experiences we wish to relive later, but he emphasizes that all soundscapes whether natural, urban, or rural possess extraordinary evocative powers. His thesis fights a hard battle; like the photographs in one's family album, no outsider is ever as moved as the person who took them, just as some may not be as moved by a recording as the person who was at a site and recorded its marvelous sounds. Yet, I urge you to take Krause at his word: go out and buy the equipment with which to make your own recordings, and record ambient sounds whenever you are in places you wish to remember. And do this until you are as reflexive about making such recordings as all of us are about taking pictures whenever we find ourselves in places we wish to remember. Krause is right: ambient sounds will get you back to such a place more vividly than any photograph ever can...and they will do so more effectively than you can imagine.

Krause also explores how non-industrial cultures have always depended "on the integrity of undisturbed natural sound for determining a *sense of place.*" He cites the BaBenzele (Bayaka) Pygmies who live in the Central African Republic, as an example. When separated from the forest, these people "become physically and mentally stressed and overwhelmed." Krause claims that "natural soundscapes are a physical and spiritual elixir." In contrast, he discusses our noisy modern world as exemplified in the crowds who are drawn to drag races by "the power of noise." He notes, "The louder the sounds we can produce, the more virile we are supposed to feel, absent anything else of consequence that provides us with a sense of self-or spiritual worth."

Krause, like me, prefers it quiet. As he says, "Listening to creature sounds, water trickling in a stream, wind in the trees, and waves at the seashore immediately puts me at ease…Yet, this miraculous biophony— this concerto of the natural world—is now under serious threat of complete annihilation." He makes a strong plea for the critical importance of conserving the acoustic integrity of such places. I predict that this book will become an important voice in support of preserving natural soundscapes.

There are chapters encouraging novice sound recordists to discover unusual things to record, such as singing sand dunes or barnacles moving within their shells. For those who get caught by the recording bug, he suggests grand projects, such as following the route of Lewis and Clark's journey from St. Louis to the Pacific, recording all the way. Or, perhaps, a recording trip that acoustically follows the 1,700-mile journey of Chief Joseph of the Nez Perce tribe, beginning in northeastern Oregon, over the Lolo Pass in Idaho, south through the Bitterroot valley, across Yellowstone, and ending at the Bear Paw Battlefield in Montana near the Canadian border. It is difficult to imagine a better way to satisfy a twin interest in history and the outdoors. This is a new way to think about planning a vacation.

There is also a useful section on troubleshooting the problems you will encounter with field recording equipment. His final, excellent advice to someone whose equipment has completely broken down and can't be fixed: "Take a deep breath and enjoy the view. Electronic equipment fails sometimes." Other practical advice includes the admonition never to use insect repellent containing the chemical DEET because "it dissolves everything."

Wild Soundscapes features a wonderful section about where to go to record lovely natural soundscapes. It includes such interesting details, as a great place to see a specific pack of wolves, as well as an aside on President Reagan's infamous comment that, "If you've seen one redwood, you've seen them all." Krause's experience points to just the opposite. Traveling all over the world to record, and comparing what sounds he has been able to capture, Krause says, "They all sound different…if you've heard one beach, you've (only) heard the unique geophony of one beach."

We are late in being able to understand the natural world through sound. Krause points out that, until quite recently, we had no way to store or reproduce sound. Thanks to the more artistic of our cave dwelling ancestors, we know what woolly mammoths looked like eons ago. If those same ancestors had been able to record sound, we would also know what they sounded like. Imagine experiencing a recording of a woolly mammoth trumpeting in the forest outside the cave. What an evocation of a distant time and place.

What Krause's book is calling for is a whole new way of interpreting our world. For that reason and many others, this is a book I recommend you buy, read, and act upon.

Contents of the Compact Disc

Introduction

Learning How to Listen

White camellias

falling —

The only sound

in the

moonlit evening

—Ranko

 The day I arrived at this spot two weeks ago, snow had covered the meadow. Now I sit amid sprouting wildflowers. Trickling water etches traceries through the snow that melts along the forest's edge. Birds nest on the newly exposed grasses; the Lincoln sparrows are so unruffled by my presence that I can walk about without upsetting any of the nesting females. Everywhere, there are nests full of eggs settled in tufts of grass and among the low bushes and trees around my campsite. I feel like when I was a teenager: hopeful, trusting, and full of dreams. Listening engages me totally, makes me feel alive and at peace. I wait a while, seduced and intoxicated by the numinous sounds. Only then do I remember to switch on my recorder, hoping to capture on tape the soundscape that reaches my ears. Streams are among the most difficult natural sounds to record; more often

•

than not, recorded streams sound nothing like the pure, radiant expression that we experience by simply listening. I've spent the last several days exploring just the right aural perspectives to mix into a soundscape composition that will evoke this magical place. My ears have become so attuned to the serene natural world that when I think of returning to the city, my mind conjures up noise. I find myself resisting the need to leave. It is the same every time I journey into the field.

Journal entry — Lincoln Meadow at
Yuba Pass, California

Wild Soundscapes is not a guidebook or instruction manual in the traditional sense. Most guidebooks provide detailed descriptions of trails and paths and depict the flora, fauna, and terrain of a city or outdoor area that you might want to visit. Such books focus on the physical features one may *see*. Instead, this book is a resource for exploring new ways to experience the wild through your ability *to hear*. You will learn techniques for listening and interpreting, discovering what you can't hear by ears alone, and experimenting with natural sound recording. By trying out some of the exercises in this book and strengthening your interpretive skills, you may find that your overall sense of the world's presence has dramatically changed.

This book will teach you how to listen to the voices of the natural world. Use the glossary at the end of the book for terms you don't know. Skip around to sections that most interest you. Use the compact disc at the back of the book to enhance your understanding of natural sound and sound recording techniques.

This book is also about the language we use to describe what we hear, and the limitations of our philosophies, education, and the concepts that have evolved to inform us about wildness. I use the phrase *wild natural* when speaking of the collective voice of creatures and the habitats in which they dwell. "Nature" is an overused and abstract word, intertwined with a tradition that has created an "it/us" dichotomy that separates us from the very world we try to describe. Many cultures that live more simply and closer to the earth do not even have a separate word for "nature."

Ironically, awareness of the sounds of earth and its creatures is one of the last frontiers of discovery in our scientifically oriented culture. We are somewhat late in coming to an understanding of the natural world through sound and have to re-learn what our ancestors knew millions of years ago. For those who know how to deeply listen to their natural surroundings, new discoveries are being made almost every day. Our aural territories are exciting to explore; they lead us to breakthroughs in the way we understand the natural world and our interdependent and complex relationships within it.

You can experience the collective voices of the natural world simply through unaided listening with your ears. Or, you can enhance and expand your ability to listen and decipher natural soundscapes through the use of kid-simple and accessible amplification or recording gear. I first heard natural sound enhanced by a microphone and a pair of earphones over 30 years ago in a wooded area north of San Francisco. The epiphany was so overwhelming that I completely lost track of time and was oblivious that darkness had fallen. When I realized it was time to return to the road where I had parked, I found myself alone and apprehensive in an unfamiliar world. Stumbling down a couple of miles of unmarked trails without a flashlight, I finally reached the spot where I had parked my car. This was my first experience venturing alone into an unpopulated habitat and I was embarrassed by how little I knew about my environment and how to survive in it.

I set out to improve my ability to listen to the voices of the natural world but quickly discovered that there were no resources to guide me. Now, after several decades of listening in the field, working as a *bioacoustician** and natural sound recordist, I have learned many lessons and have tips to share. Mostly, I want to impart my passion for this work and my concerns about what the wild natural is trying to tell us. It is critical that we pay attention to these expressive soundscapes. So, while you are having fun learning new listening skills, you will also learn a lot about creatures, habitats, and how humans, noise, natural sound and various environments all impact one another.

⋰⟩ Quick Facts on Natural Sound

In 1968 it took 15 recording hours to get one hour's worth of natural sound, usable in a professional recording. Now, due to human noise and disturbed habitats, it takes about 2,000 recording hours to get the same result.

About 2 percent of our old-growth forests remain standing in the Lower Forty-eight states, down from 45 percent just thirty years ago.

The United States accounts for 5 percent of the global population, yet uses well over half of our planet's natural resources.

Over 25 percent of the North American natural soundscapes in my archives were recorded in habitats that have since become extinct; many vital natural soundscapes no longer exist—except on tape.

---

*Words in **bold italic** are defined in "Some Terms Used in this Book" on page 151.

The first time I heard a spring dawn chorus listening through head-phones attached to microphones, I immediately realized that with my ears, alone, I had been missing an exquisite part of the nature sound experience. Amplified sound gave me a way to translate the language of the natural world in ways my "civilized" ears could not grasp. The experience re-trained my hearing so that I now perceive through a sharpened aural acu-ity something approaching what our forest-dwelling ancestors might have known (or at least I like to think this is so). The song of life reached me with a force so great that my world was forever transformed: *heightened listening was the key*.

Many of us do not distinguish between the two acts of listening and hearing. It's one thing to hear…quite another to be able to listen. The first obstacle I had to overcome in my learning curve was simply my inability to *listen*. Although my ears *heard* sound, they were not trained to distinguish the many subtleties present in the world of natural sound. Listening through headphones and microphones taught me how to attend more care-fully. Microphones, or **mics** as they are casually referred to in the profession, amplify sound in certain concentrated ways. They accelerate your ability to listen carefully. A mic lets you differentiate between what to listen *to* and what to listen *for* in much the same way that a microscope, telescope, or pair of binoculars can increase your ability to focus on, identify, and observe visual elements of the world. Through headphones and microphones, you hear pieces of the aural fabric in such gloriously clear detail that you will be surprised by what you have been missing. You will also become more cog-nizant of things and situations to avoid when you are wanting to experience natural and wild settings, discovering all too poignantly that it is quite dif-ficult to find places of "pure" natural sound. Our experience of the wild nat-ural is constantly interrupted by the sounds of machinery, airplanes, trains and cars, as well as the barking and mooing of our domesticated animals.

You can learn to listen in an *active* rather than passive way. A keen awareness of, and involvement in, the fascinating world of living sound can be achieved by anyone willing to learn how to become a *careful* listener. The joy is that the learning is so much fun! Living sound surrounds us. Our awareness of it intensifies our connection to life and makes us better able to survive and flourish within our native environments. Nevertheless, the nat-ural world is slow to reveal its secrets and few are trained to listen with the kind of attention needed.

For most modern industrialized people, hearing has become a blur. As much of the world population shifted from agrarian to industrial economies, the local folk knew that their aural environment was being transformed: railroads and factories drastically altered the land—and soundscapes—and we were on our way to the machine age and all of its attendant noise.

Noise is the cacophony of unpleasant or harsh sounds human beings have created by our ruthless pace, our machinery, and even our toys. It has increased tremendously in our living environments and even permeates our recreational activities, thus masking more aesthetically pleasing and resonant sounds. One result of increased noise levels is an increase in our physiological level of stress. Unfortunately, we have adapted to the higher volume of our environment over the centuries, and have come to endure a culture of noise. Not without consequences, however. Many of us are seriously listening-challenged, hearing-impaired, or tone deaf to those very elements that might enchant and nurture or stimulate and soothe us. There is even evidence to demonstrate that people who live within cultures where there is little human-induced industrial or mechanical noise, have a far smaller incidence of hearing loss.[1]

We have come to endure a type of experience in the natural world akin to going to a movie whose subject follows one plot, while the sound tells another, conflicting story. For instance, the sounds of snowmobiles in Yellowstone completely obliterate the serene peacefulness that would otherwise be present during the winter months, thus thwarting the intended purpose of a wild sanctuary or natural park: what is less natural than a high-decibel snowmobile ripping up the local countryside? It is as if our civilization dispensed with sound as a vital part of our experience—almost as if it doesn't matter or exist at all. You would never think of going to a movie theater outfitted with a Dolby Digital or THX system and turning off the sound. Why should it be different with our experience of the natural world? The experience of natural sound adds a vibrant and palpable dimension to our visual encounters.

The first time you experience the natural world's creature choruses through techniques and tools described in this book, you might be bewildered by what seems to be the disorganized and unexpected quality of sound. What seems chaotic at first is generally the result of our inexperience or inability to comprehend the complex patterns of sound that reveal themselves as we spend more time within the fold of the natural world. Stephen Jay Gould, Harvard professor and popular science writer, has suggested that human beings have great difficulty grasping larger, more complex concepts even when they may hold the keys to simpler truths. We have a situation where "the invisibility of larger contexts [is] caused by too much focus upon single items, otherwise known as missing the forest through the trees."[2] Sound comes to us in a combination of both fixed and variable expressions simultaneously. Robins will always sing in my backyard in the spring. This is an established, predictable event that I experience every year. However, they sing from different trees at different distances and in different numbers: the variable. Because our experience of listening to the voices of the wild natural is so new, we know very little about what these creature sounds convey. However, by training ourselves to listen more attentively, we can begin to identify—within the larger context of natural soundscapes

—indicators that may prove helpful to our understanding of the wild natural.

I can't imagine living without the divine music of the natural world enveloping me. Enjoying and finding comfort in this symphony of natural sound has had a major impact on my life; it has led to many marvels and satisfying insights. This book is an effort to bring those miracles into your world. As you learn to really listen, you can transform the everyday moment-by-moment experiences of your life and benefit in a number of unexpected ways. So many urban situations directly increase anxiety, and noise level is a chief culprit causing panic, hypervigilance, anger, and nervous tension. The sounds of the creature world, on the other hand, of water trickling down a stream, wind in the trees, and waves at the seashore can immediately put us at ease. Most of us relax and slow down when we get away from the noise of cities, phones, and the ever-present sounds of electronic media. We breathe more deeply, take in more oxygen, strengthen our sensory apparatus, and replenish our frayed synapses. At some point, many of us come to recognize a deep need to actively support the preservation of quietude and work to protect natural sound wherever it remains intact. Thus, the popularity of rain sticks, meditation retreats, living room water fountains, and well-produced natural soundscape recordings.

The kind of active and considered listening I propose is quiet and gentle. It is designed to create a new understanding, a gathering of kindred spirits, human and otherwise, which can lead to discoveries about how we all make our presence known. If we select the right places to listen and wait —patiently—we might find that the creature world has stories to divulge that are nothing short of amazing. As our connection to the wild natural increases, we will be moved to learn more, preserve, and protect the vulnerable habitats where these sounds still remain vital and intact.

1. Schafer, R. Murray. *The Book of Noise.* (Indian River, Ontario: Arcana Editions, 1998.)

2. Gould, Stephen Jay. "Abolish the Recent," in *Natural History Magazine.* (American Academy of Science: New York, NY, May 1991), pp. 16–21.

CHAPTER 1

The Mystery of Sound

With the sense of sight, the idea communicates the emotion,

whereas, with sound, the emotion communicates the idea,

which is more direct and therefore more powerful.

—Alfred North Whitehead

 Hearing is the most mysterious of all our human senses. Sound cannot be seen, touched, or smelled. What John Spong, author and former Episcopal Bishop of Newark, New Jersey, says of trying to characterize God, perfectly applies to the magic of sound: "While it can be experienced, it can never be defined."[1] We need to take on faith that the content of what we hear in the natural wild is not only fascinating and incredibly rich in detail, but absolutely vital to our lives and our survival. Nothing can replace it.

The ear is a magical receptor, capable of processing far more complex information than we had ever thought possible. Through the operation of the ear and the brain together, we are linked to information we may never fully comprehend. Every natural sound tells a detailed and eloquent story. Living organisms, human and non-human, guided by the resonant messages of their respective habitats, are informed by the transforming secrets revealed in natural sounds.

Because it is remarkably intimate and immediate, sound is perhaps the most influential of our senses. *Sound wave* energy, whether it is generated by human speech or microwave ovens, is so physical it actually heats the space in which it is transmitted. Think of all the knowledge and emotion communicated through the medium of sound. It can inform or elevate us, make us feel sad, inspired or soothed. It can agitate us, create a sense of serene tranquility, or evoke mental pictures.

Sound is also key to enjoying much of our entertainment: try to watch "Star Wars" with the soundtrack turned off or imagine a world without Bach or Beethoven, Lightnin' Hopkins or Miles Davis, Kathleen Battle or Emmy Lou Harris. However, the use of loud sound design to create excitement or suspense, or to represent action, drama, and power often leads to something more like *cacophony*, so intense and distracting that even the loudest wild creature's voice is drowned out. Some sounds, such as prolonged exposure to loud and distorted noise, can actually cause physical harm. On the other hand, research is being done on sounds that can contribute to a process of healing.[2]

What is Sound?

Sound is essentially the sensation we get when our nervous system's auditory center is stimulated. The source of the stimulation is a pattern of cyclical waves of pressure that are generated by any sound-producing mechanism. These waves are then transmitted through the air at a high enough rate or *frequency* and at a high and loud enough level or *amplitude* to be detected by our ears. Once received, these waves of sound energy are translated at the auditory centers of our brains into impressions of sound.

The extraordinary and complex mechanism of the human ear allows us to discriminate between extremely fine details within the texture of sound. Even those of us with some hearing impairment can distinguish the sound of one human voice from another. Not only do we have an innate ability to distinguish between individual human voices, we also possess a latent aptitude that allows us to hear patterns of sound among less familiar voices such as those expressed in the natural world. Creature voices define a habitat within certain larger environments and can cue us toward new insights into our experience of the wild.[3] Nevertheless, the ability to hear the wild natural in discriminating ways has not been much used since we, as a civilization, became industrialized. Learning to use this gift once again is a process of discovery that is exciting, easy, and great fun.

Two Types of Sound

Sound in the human world is categorized in two ways: desirable and undesirable. These are differentiated in the field of *bioacoustics* as useful *information* as opposed to *noise*. We often don't notice noise, what author Joachim–Ernst Berendt refers to in his book, *The Third Ear*, as "…acoustic garbage," when hearing with our ears alone. Yet, our brains are at work filtering out undesirable sounds so that we can better hear and process what is beneficial or useful.

We have all had the experience of talking with a companion in a noisy restaurant or on a crowded urban street. As we gaze at the source of the sound, we think we are hearing everything perfectly. However, what we hear is mostly *what we see*. In our auditory centers, we may be receiving many different sounds, but our brains are at work filtering out the background noise so that we think that the interference doesn't matter. This activity goes on whether or not we are fully aware of it. Even as our attention is focused on what we see, our brains are busy working overtime to retrieve, process, and transmit the desirable information. If this goes on for a prolonged time, we are subjected to varying degrees of measurable fatigue and stress, although the tolerance level may vary from individual to individual.

Some industries manipulate this process in order to trigger or reduce human stress levels. Restaurant architects and interior designers, for example, plan restaurant environments to be more or less stressful. By introducing hard, reverberant surfaces that reflect and amplify the slightest sound, they can create a noisier space. The noise triggers a stress and fatigue response that encourages quick patron turnover, resulting in higher profits for the restaurateur. Consider how relaxed you feel in a quiet eating establishment with lots of sound-absorbent material factored into the design—and how less likely you are to hurry out the door. Not good for profits to have you sitting there all evening! The *New York Times* discussed the problem of restaurant noise in a number of editorials several years ago and subsequently began to report noise levels as part of their regular restaurant reviews to allow readers to choose between noisier or quieter dining options. Some newspapers and magazines are now using small icons to identify a restaurant's noise level in their reviews.

⍁ Try This!

Select an environment that is familiar to you. Bring along a microphone and a recorder and after setting it up, hit the "record" button. Focus on something as simple as a conversation in the quiet of your home without any background noise (refrigerators, ringing telephones, entertainment centers, cars passing outside, dogs barking, plumbing, etc.). Or, try a place outdoors, such as a neighborhood park or footpath. Play back your recording later on. After this experience, your way of listening will begin to change.

The presence of unwanted noise becomes most apparent when we introduce a microphone and recorder into the environment. Microphones, as an extension of our ears, do not discriminate between useful sounds and noise. They pick up *everything* that produces sound within the given range of their design. If you want to know how much noise there is in an environment, just plug a mic into a recorder and put on a set of headphones.

Research on Noise

There is still not much available research on noise and its impact on human and other organisms. The area of study to draw the most attention has been focused on the relationship between extremely high decibel exposures and hearing loss. An intriguing study that linked noise and stress levels took place in the early 1980s in Strasbourg, France. Researchers invited three young men and three women to sleep in a specially designed laboratory where they were subjected to different sound and noise experiences each night over a period of several weeks. Wired to instrumentation that registered heart rate, finger-pulse amplitude, and pulse-wave velocity, each test subject was monitored for stress levels throughout the night. On the first few nights, the team enjoyed uninterrupted quiet, followed by two weeks in which the researchers played recordings of traffic noise. Upon waking, participants completed questionnaires detailing their experiences.

All stress indicators dramatically increased when the traffic noise was *first* introduced. After two to seven nights of noise, however, the subjects reported that they were no longer aware of being disturbed. Each person had become used to it. Yet, the physiological stress levels measured by the instrumentation indicated the same consistently high numbers as noted on the first night when the traffic sounds were introduced.[4] While the minds of the subjects rationalized that there was no noise issue, their bodies told a very different story.

Loss of Natural Sound

Natural sound is no longer the primary material most of us in industrial cultures use to gather knowledge about our environment. We tend to be suspicious and fearful of experiences in the natural world that are not easy to explain or quantify. Many people completely avoid or shy away from contact with the wild. There is a large-scale devaluation of natural sounds in part because they are so elusive and "foreign" to us. We are intimidated by such encounters.[5] Yet, at some point in our distant past, our species intimately knew the natural places where we lived—as much by sound as by sight and scent. Knowledge of our surrounding natural world was balanced between what we heard, saw, smelled, touched and felt kinesthetically. No single faculty dominated the others.

When human beings shifted from hunting and gathering cultures to more settled agrarian ones, we built villages and cities to conduct trade, house ourselves, and localize our festivals and religious rites. More stable food supplies and expanding urban centers led to increased populations around the globe; beliefs and attitudes about the natural world changed, along with our relationship to natural sounds and noise. Control over what we viewed as "Nature" became essential, and Nature became something outside ourselves with which we needed to contend. Along with this major shift in human societies, animals were domesticated, and new inventions came into being: waterwheels to power mills, blacksmithing to pound iron into tools, and cart wheels to carry our supplies over cobblestone streets. Every new invention symbolized industriousness and progress, yet inevitably altered the environmental soundscape.

At the dawn of the Industrial Revolution, attitudes about our place in the natural world began to change more rapidly. We proudly equated noise with advancements in civilization. As more human noise was introduced into our environments, inevitably masking natural sounds, our connection to the wild natural began to recede into memories accompanied by a vague discomfort, nostalgia, and a more forceful sense of loss often articulated by the poets of the time.

> *Sometimes, when a bird cries out,*
> *Or the wind sweeps through a tree,*
> *Or a dog howls in a far-off farm,*
> *I hold still and listen a long time.*
>
> *My world turns and goes back to the place*
> *Where, a thousand forgotten years ago,*
> *The bird and the blowing wind*
> *Were like me, and were my brothers.*
>
> *My soul turns into a tree,*
> *And an animal, and a cloud bank.*
> *Then changed and odd it comes home*
> *And asks me questions. What should I reply?*

> —Hermann Hesse

As population centers continued to grow in the next few hundred centuries up until our own time, a large-scale alteration of natural areas into agricultural and industrial production profoundly transformed most of the planet's landscapes. Almost imperceptibly at first, with each passing century, more land went into production at an increasing rate. Parallel with this change, attitudes about the wild natural also became more distorted and were expressed through fear and alienation as humans became increasingly separated from their ancient natural roots. Philosophies and cultural institutions changed as civilizations grew in social and economic complexity. Interpretation of religious doctrine in the West held that Nature was, indeed, something to subdue and dominate. To my mind, that included the "wild" (creative) in human nature, as well. Fear about natural sound was even transferred to attitudes about musical expression. For example, in the late 15th century, Savanarola, a dictator-monk living in Florence, concluded that the sixth note in the musical scale was "the Devil's music." Citizens were barbecued *á la Jean d'Arc* if they were discovered producing that particular tone. While some sounds were deemed offensive to the Church, other types of musical sound and styles were condoned. Many late Medieval and Renaissance thinkers found spiritual significance in the "music of the spheres," the harmonic sound made by the rhythm of the planets and stars according to Divine Plan, as well as a Pythagorean speculation on the relation of whole numbers to musical consonances.[6] However, the high Renaissance notion of a Great Chain of Being elevated human beings above all other species which meant that voices within the fold of the natural world were no longer valued as intrinsic to the well-being or cultivation of human society. The European scientific revolution and period of Enlightenment went even further in delimiting the importance of the creature world.

Dominance of the Visual

Much of human culture, particularly as our civilization developed in the West, has sprung from the physical information we gained from the *observable* cues of our world. Until recently we did not have a way to store or reproduce natural sounds, whereas we have had the ability and technologies to represent nature in visual images ever since the Paleolithic period. Some 40,000 years ago, we discovered that we could capture the image of a gazelle, mammoth, goat or bull on cave walls and stony outcrops.

The graphic image was the dominant force in how we understood our real and imagined realms, becoming central to the ways we experienced our legends, histories, spiritual stories and personal identities. Where collections of images were created, they came to be revered, either as religious icons or as pieces of art displayed solemnly in silent museums. While the sciences historically emphasized visual observation and abstraction as the truest method for perceiving the world, many of our most valued forms of artistic expression also emphasized what could be perceived and represented *visually*. Sound could not be reproduced or stored until the late nineteenth century with Thomas Edison's first recorder. As our energies went toward the visible world, our other senses were left behind, thus changing our perception of the wild natural which diverged into numerous forms of representation and abstraction ever since.

The Jivaro

As we strayed from a balanced use of our senses within the natural world, our ability to listen in the discriminating ways of our ancestors was seriously impaired. I had a personal experience of discovering this when I spent time in the Amazon Basin with the Jivaro. Inspired by an article I had seen, I visited this indigenous tribe in 1984. The Jivaro live in the Amazon Basin much as they have for several thousand years, except they no longer make a practice of ensnaring enemies, shrinking their heads, and cooking up the more tender parts as a meal. The Jivaro helped re-orient my thoughts about the powers inherent in natural sound and led me to some insights into what our ancestors once knew about hearing and understanding their forest retreats.

One evening I was invited to join the men of the tribe on a traditional hunt. We traveled under the forest canopy without flashlights, torches, starlight or moonlight. There was nothing to direct us except the *sound*. Guided only by the delicate fabric of the **biophony**, the symbiotic relationship of sound made by birds, mammals, insects and amphibians as they vocalized together, we made our way through unseeable territory.

At first all I heard was a din. To the Jivaro, however, the forest habitat seemed exquisitely defined. They knew how to listen to it. The Jivaro tribesmen could distinguish the sounds of the rainforest as though they were being transmitted in a kind of creature Morse Code formulated out of discrete and intelligible patterns of sound and filled with useful information. The acute patterns of the aural environment guided the hunters in the general direction of their prey and eventually pinpointed the game's precise location. Surrounded by complete darkness, the hunters knew what creatures lurked down the path and whether or not these organisms qualified as prey worthy of the hunt or as threats needing to be avoided. The forest soundscape itself served as a finely-gauged global-positioning system (GPS) for them. They also enjoyed the added advantage of being able to interpret the vast quantities of aural data much in the same way that sightless humans can learn to skillfully navigate urban territory by relying on sound, smell, touch and memory.

As I stumbled through the rainforest that night, it struck me that much of humanity had experienced a tremendous loss when it turned to the world of the visual for our most important information. I wanted to relearn the skills that my friends in the Amazon forest still held sacred.

Recovering the world of sound

The late Pitzer College scientist and professor, Paul Shepard, argued that we are still connected to that ancient voice of the forest or desert. He suggested that the human genetic code has not changed since we emerged as *sapiens* from the Pleistocene.[7] Our knowledge of indigenous cultures like those of the Jivaro, the BaBenzele (Bayaka) Pygmies in the Central African Republic, the Kaluli of New Guinea, and the Pitjanjara of the Australian outback, is teaching us about the relationships these peoples have to the soundscapes of their respective worlds. There are remarkable similarities in the ways these cultures connect to the wild natural and living sound. From them, we may hear an echo of our own history and lost wisdom.

Anthropologists and archaeologists are bringing to light new clues about where we came from and who we are as they understand how other cultures of both the present and near-distant past made sense of the world. Natural soundscapes furnished not only the roots of language, but the foundation of music, long before we began to worship pictographs and petroglyphs. The animals in our desert and forest environments were the ones who taught us to dance and sing as we mimicked and shadowed their elegant movements and voices. If we wish to hear that creature orchestra again, we have to slow down, become very quiet and listen intently. Perhaps we need to use some new technologies to enhance our experience and retrain our ears. Of all the issues surrounding natural soundscapes, none is more pressing than that of *quietude*—the reduction of unwanted noise in our environments.

1. Spong, John Shelby. *A New Christianity for a New World: Why Traditional Faith Is Dying and How a New Faith Is Being Born*. (Harper Collins: San Francisco, 2001.)

2. Berger, E.H., Royster, L.H., Royster, J.D., Driscoll, D.P., Layne, M. *The Noise Manual*, 5th edition. (American Industrial Hygiene Association Press: Fairfax, VA, 2000.)

3. Krause, B. *Into a Wild Sanctuary*. (Heyday Books: Berkeley, CA, 1998.)

4. *Science News*, Volume 121. June 5, 1982, p. 380.

5. Abram, David. *Awakening What's Wild Within Us*. (Wild Earth, Milkweed Press: Minneapolis, MN, 2002.)

6. Helmholtz, Hermann. *On the Sensations of Tone*. (Dover Publications: Mineola, NY, 1954; first published in English in 1875.)

7. Shepard, Paul. *Coming Home to the Pleistocene*. (Island Press: Washington, D.C., 1998.)

CHAPTER 2

Land of Noise

Making Peace with Quiet

One day man will have to combat noise

as he once combated cholera and the plague.

—Robert Koch

 One eerie and yet remarkable effect that resulted from the security precautions put in place after the horrendous disaster of September 11, 2001, was the incredible quiet that ascended above our small Northern California county. Our home is located directly below the flight path of planes arriving from all over the world and making their final descents into San Francisco International Airport, located approximately 60 miles to the south. Because air traffic was grounded for a few days, no jet planes flew over our house. As my wife, Katherine, and I sat in the garden under the stars the evening after the attacks in New York and Washington, we could hear owls and insects that we had never heard at that time of year. At one point, we remarked that we felt *guilty* for appreciating the absence of the jet noise and the roar of smaller aircraft, and helicopters. We sat there stunned by the previous day's events and the silence and wondered aloud about the possibilities of the nation slowing down, catching our collective breath, and appreciating the wonderful natural blessings we can otherwise enjoy in our own backyards.

I have found that I like it *quiet*. When I was a child, my parents took me and my sister to a snow-covered valley in Yellowstone National Park one winter. From where we stood, a mysterious and powerful silence engulfed

us; a silence that was only occasionally punctuated by the calls, cries and chirps of ravens, jays, magpies, and horned larks. Elk, deer, and other four-legged creatures were drawn to the lower elevations for protection and the expectation of food, which meant that we could easily spot them and sometimes hear their voices. In recent years, this enchanting experience has been shattered by the relentless presence of snowmobiles racing through the valley. The magical quiet is shattered in an instant, obliterated by engine noise and smog. In Grand Canyon National Park, noise from tourist flights or the whistling tourist steam train traveling along the rim, breaks into any awestruck reverie one might otherwise enjoy standing above or below the chasm. In California's great Mojave Desert, dune buggies and dirt bikes fracture the peacefulness. We live in an increasingly noisy world, so much so that many of us now have heard the term *noise pollution* and have heard about efforts being made to combat it.

Have Noise, Will Travel

We seem to bring noise with us wherever we go: to high mountain lakes, we bring jet skis and motor boats; to the sea-shore, we bring boom boxes; to the woods, we bring dirt bikes and chain saws; to the desert, we bring radios and dune buggies. It seems that no matter where we try to find relief from the din of our lives, unwanted noise intrudes. So much noise encroaches on our lives, we sometimes can't even hear one another!

The powerful materialism that symbolizes the American dream of prosperity and freedom may be at the very heart of our noise problem. As a nation, we are preoccupied with power and with the machinery that provides a sense of might. Many people in policy positions share James Watt's view that, "noise and power go hand in hand." Watt, former Secretary of the Interior under President Ronald Reagan, considered this to be a good thing, a sign of national strength and progress. How this belief gets dramatized—even in our recreational activities—can be found in a number of arenas. The first one, unfortunately, is too close to home. On any July Sunday afternoon, huge crowds are drawn to the power of speed and noise at Sears Point, a famous NASCAR drag-racing site located 18 miles south of our home. Yet, the roar of the engines emanating from each race event does not travel in a straight line. It must first traverse several ranges of coastal hills, valleys, protected wetlands, and a state park before it arrives at our ears. It does this at measurable and troubling levels as each contest begins every five minutes or so. The engines of the dragsters are so loud that I have recorded them on tape well above the normal daytime ambient levels present where we live.

In another example, a sound industry manufacturer's award was given in the year 2000 for the loudest sound system ever produced for the interior of an automobile environment. To hold the attention of young consumers, a music system was designed that could generate a sound pressure level of 174dBA. This means it has nearly a factor of 2 louder than a .357 magnum pistol being shot off at your ear, and a factor of 7 louder than if you were standing on the runway ten yards from a Boeing 747 at full take-off power. And, all of this happens *inside* a car!

A final example comes from the movies. Sound levels in movie theaters with THX or Dolby Digital systems now approach a factor of 6 greater than they did a decade ago—often beyond what the Environmental Protection Agency deems as a safe industrial noise level. "The public demands it," is the film industry's justification for these increases. I just take earplugs when my wife and I go to the movies these days.

Why is it that with all our technological objectives of making human life more comfortable, we haven't designed mechanical equipment to be more quiet? Could it be that we create this noise to supplant the voices we've silenced in the natural world? Paul Shepard theorized that certain signs of pathological human behavior are directly related to the loss of wild habitat and our disconnection to the natural world. To him, the ever-increasing and unwanted noise in our culture was an expression of power. Shepard lamented the significant loss of creature voices over the course of his twentieth-century lifetime as he described the important roles natural soundscapes play in our lives.[1]

Canadian composer R. Murray Schafer is another contemporary intellectual who observed that human-induced noise not only contributes to soundscape loss in the wild but also represents a potentially destructive form of power. In *The Book of Noise*, he suggests that our noise-producing symbols of brawn—pile-drivers, front-loaders, jet aircraft, for example—overwhelm and supersede the voices of the natural world, including organisms of all sizes, as well as thunder, wind, ocean waves and the shaking of the earth itself.

We Will, We Will, Rock You

That human noises have a direct impact on the natural world could not be made more clear than in the following incident. In 1999, the *Los Angeles Times* reported that rock diva Tina Turner's voice had been identified as the most effective way to scare off birds who were hanging around the runways of England's Gloucestershire Airport. Airport staff had previously used recordings of avian distress calls and the cries of predators to frighten away birds that were settling on the airport's landing strips. They had encountered a limited success with these methods. When they switched to playing loud recordings of the famed rock singer, there was an immediate and dramatic reduction in the number of birds that interfered with the landings and departures of corporate jets, helicopters, and other aircraft.

Human noise can greatly impair the transmission and reception of natural soundscapes, and dramatically affect the behavior of wildlife and humans, alike. Even the behavior of otherwise wild creatures held in captivity is greatly affected by their urban soundscape environments. In 1993, when a military jet buzzed Sweden's Froso Zoo, about 300 miles north of Stockholm, during a routine training flight, the tigers, lynx, and foxes panicked.[2] Some of the animals tore apart and ate twenty-three of their babies, including five rare Siberian tiger cubs. Trying to protect their offspring from the onslaught of noise, the animals resorted to infanticide.

Little is known about how wild creatures receive and process combinations of noise and otherwise relevant aural information in their natural habitats or about how random noise events might affect a particular natural soundscape. Yet, evidence of an increasing and measurable loss of natural sound and the damage that noise inflicts on creature habitats has started to come to light. The relatively slow pace of research has largely been the

result of two factors: inferior technology necessary to do the studies, and a general lack of interest. New bioacoustic field research is showing patterns that reveal a loss of biophony due to noise, something that field recordists have been sensitive to for some time. The loss of natural sound and its inevitable effect on the surviving organisms may be more profound than scientists had earlier thought.

Soundscapes

Pure natural soundscapes, places where no human noise is present, often feature a glorious symphony of creature and non-creature voices. As human clamor increases and habitats shrink, non-human sounds have become difficult to hear or have been muted altogether. Animal survival often depends on the numerous ways in which creatures vocalize in their particular habitats. When unwanted noise is present, human and non-human creatures, alike, are denied the soundscape experience of the wild natural. Humans, especially, lose that positive interaction between them-selves and that world. In the next chapter, we will further explore just what creature soundscapes are and how we can recover our links to them.

The concepts of soundscape and *acoustic ecology* were first brought into our common language by R. Murray Schafer in a book titled *Tuning of the World*. In another work *Je n'ai jamais vu un son* (*I Never Saw a Sound*), Schafer reminds us of our own creation myth:

> *En premier lieu, Dieu parla; en second lieu, il vit que cela était bon. Chez les créateurs, le son précède toujours la vue tout comme chez les êtres vivants l'ouie précède la vue. Il in fut ainsi pour les premièr créatures de la terre: et il en est toujours ainsi pour le nouveau-né.*

> (God spoke first and saw that it was good second. Among the creators, sounding always precedes seeing, just as among the created, hearing pre-cedes vision. It was that way with the first creatures on earth and still is with the new-born babe.)

The term *soundscape* refers to any acoustic environment, whether it springs from natural, urban, or rural sources. It takes into account all of the sound present at any given time. Shafer and his assistant, Barry Truax, introduced the concept of *acoustic ecology* in the late 1970s during the World Soundscape Project conducted at Simon Fraser University in Vancouver, British Columbia. It refers to the field of study concerned with the relationships between soundscapes and listeners, and how the nature of these relationships characterize the quality of any given urban, rural, or natural soundscape.[3] The World Forum for Acoustic Ecology and other organizations continue to explore this innovative field. While biophony is a type of soundscape confined to the sounds that organisms generate in a particular habitat, *geophony* is a soundscape of non-living phenomena, for instance, the sound of streams, storms, wind through trees or across sands, eruptions and earthquakes, and a myriad other natural causes.

As human-induced noise, in particular, impairs the transmission and reception of natural soundscapes, it has become evident that there is a clear need to create a quieter civilization. In the next chapter, we will explore just exactly what creature soundscapes, or biophonies, are and how we can recover our links to them.

1. Shepard, Paul. *Nature & Madness*. (University of Georgia Press: Athens, GA, 1998.)

2. *San Francisco Chronicle*, September 18, 1999; distributed by *Los Angeles Times* Syndicate.

3. Schafer, R. Murray. *The Tuning of the World*. (Alfred A. Knopf: New York, NY, 1977.)

CHAPTER 3

Biophony

Soundscapes in the Natural World

Any living thing which triumphs in the struggle

against its environment destroys itself.

—Gregory Bateson

 Elders in the Wy-am tribe tell of a time that they fished all year long at Celilo Falls, a little west of the Columbia River's midway point. Each season brought with it lots of fish, including spring Chinook salmon, summer Chinook, bluebacks, fall Chinook, steelhead and coho. When the catch was good, members could harvest a ton of fish a day—soon having enough to supply close and extended family with all that they needed for a year with little more than the cost of a couple of balls of twine. In recent history a major event took place along the Columbia River in the Pacific Northwest. It went unnoticed by most of the media, but it profoundly affected those who had lived in the region for thousands of years.

On the morning of March 10, 1957, the Army Corps of Engineers ordered the massive steel gates of the newly built Dalles Dam shut, strangling the natural downstream flow of the river. As the Elders stood on the river bank astonished, a way of life that had sustained them for centuries disappeared in less than a day. It all happened very quickly. Six hours later and eight miles upstream, the sacred site of the Wy-am was completely submerged. That day, there wasn't a dry eye on the banks near Celilo, the small village on the river's edge. The Elders were not weeping for the loss of salmon. They wept because the river no longer lent its wise voice to the community. The submerged Celilo Falls were dead silent.

Learning By Ear

There is music in all things, if men had ears.

—Lord Byron

Historically, researchers in the natural sciences abstracted single components out of a larger context in an effort to better identify, quantify, and categorize individual elements and organisms. The first students of natural sound practiced the same method to bring information to light. However, much more can be learned by listening to the collective sound expressed by an entire *biome*, or habitat of these creatures. The density and texture of natural soundscapes always convey more robust information and offer more details than any single element can reveal on its own.

As a naturalist, I was formally educated in the classical manner of observation and analysis, which taught me to "see" the natural world by breaking it down into its component parts. I learned to pay particular attention to the sounds of individual birds and mammals and to distinguish one sound from another. Yet, to truly understand the relationships between components, we need to consider the aural expressions of entire habitats.

Our academic and research literature has rarely focused on the notion of the aural interdependence of vocal organisms in a given biome. In a 1977 paper on birdsong, Peter Marler and Kenneth Marten suggested the possibility that creatures vocalize in some (yet to be understood) relationship to one another.[1] In another publication, Jakob von Uexküll, a behavioral physiologist of the early 20th century, refers to the notion of *sensory niches*, in general.[2] According to some historians of the field, the latter work is considered seminal.

Going back a bit further in time, we have a record of a naturalist encountering and describing a particular biome in the writings of John Muir, the Scottish immigrant who inspired the nation's national park system. Sitting alone in the Sierra Nevada mountains, under a grove of white pines, Muir was captivated by the singular distinction of the well-tempered wing-like hum of pine needles whirring in the wind. He claimed he could tell where he was by the pine music alone, even if he were set down blindfolded anywhere in the mountains.[3] It is this method of listening that we need to relearn.

These few written records suggest that habitats have particular aural imprints, such as the one created by the drone of pine needles or the combined music of the Wy-am's homeland. They are perhaps the earliest articulations of the idea of biophony that I have found in the scientific literature. Yet, aural niches have been known throughout the ages and put to practical application by many of the world's native cultures. In our scientific literature it is only within the last century that initial inquiries were made considering the implications of this phenomenon and reviving the issue as one of importance.

The Creature Choir in Kenya

I dreamt last night that all the animals were singing together like the Mormon Tabernacle Choir. It was one of those compelling and forceful reveries that washed wave upon wave of interwoven melody and rhythm over me. The dream was one of the few I can recall and it haunts me. Could it be that we have been missing a key element in the sonic puzzle by taking the sounds of nature apart piece by piece and that the natural world is calling our attention to an expression of creature symphony we haven't wished to think about?

In 1983, on assignment in Kenya to capture natural soundscapes for an exhibit by San Francisco's California Academy of Sciences, I was situated near a popular tourist location called Governor's Camp. I had set up my microphones and recorded and spent nearly 36 hours waiting to hear an extraordinary repeat performance of the echo-y sound of hyenas vocalizing in the nearby forest. They had been loudly calling during the previous couple of nights and I was determined not to leave that location without capturing the haunting sound on tape.

Beyond the point of exhaustion, I lay on the ground half awake and listened to the mellifluous sounds of the early morning through my headphones. As if in a dream, I began to experience the creature ambiance as a musical composition rather than as a chaotic din. It seemed that all the insects, birds, bats and ground mammals were performing as instruments in a vast animal orchestra.

When I returned to San Francisco, I transferred short recorded samples from my time in Africa to a device that graphically displays them as *"voice prints"* or *spectrograms*. Patterns between the sounds of insects, birds, mammals, and amphibians were immediately evident and differentiated almost as distinctly as notes on a symphonic score. This animal symphony, the unique manner in which creatures vocalize in a symbiotic relationship to one another in any given healthy habitat, is what I call biophony.[4] Such patterns have been found in nearly every healthy habitat I have recorded since Africa. The concept of biophony is a tool for understanding many new features of wild habitats.

Biophonies are extremely hard to capture and quantify with any consistency. One problem is that what we may be hearing may not fit our traditional models of inquiry. Even ants and insect larvae in vernal pools *sing*; the components of an environment, including creature sounds, wind and water, and other elements, might be articulating their voices in unique relationships to all other aspects of that habitat. In healthy habitats, certain insects occupy one sonic zone of the creature bandwidth, while birds, mammals, and amphibians occupy other sonic zones where there is no competition. Each system has evolved in a manner that allows the distinct expression of individual voices, and lets each creature thrive as much through its sound *iteration*, or repetitions, as from any other aspect of its being. The same type of event occurs on land and within marine environments. Thus, biophony, among other things, serves as a vital gauge of a habitat's health. It conveys data about an environment's age, level of stress related to noise, and provides us with abundant and valuable new information such as why and how creatures in both the human and non-human worlds have learned to dance and sing.

Creatures "sing" using a number of different sound-producing mechanisms, including but not limited to the use of throat and larynx. They use *stridulation*, the rubbing together of body parts like legs or antennae; they oscillate their wings; chomp and crunch using mouth parts; and make sounds as they move through different media such as when creatures dig through the earth or the pith of a tree. Some organisms may possibly create sound by the signature of metabolic rates, alone.

There was a time when humans were able to "read" the stories embedded in natural soundscapes in much the same way as those histories are now disclosed in books. On land, in particular, this delicate acoustic fabric is as well defined as the notes on a page of music when examined graphically in the form of voice prints. The notion that there can be a profound effect on soundscapes by the introduction of human-induced noise has long been understood by non-industrial cultures that depend on the integrity of undisturbed natural sound for a *sense of place*, as well as for spiritual and aesthetic reasons. In fact, the very physical and mental health of many cultures—the soles of whose individual feet come in daily contact with the ground—depends on the special relationship between undisturbed natural soundscapes and themselves.

While analyzing the recordings from Africa, it became clear that the sounds on tape were more ordered than I had anticipated. At first, I simply heard the patterns more clearly. Then, with the aid of some new sound analysis software, I was able to show and articulate the hypothesis of biophony for the first time. Undisturbed biomes, what had formerly been considered by most of us as a chaotic din of noise, consist of a cohesive number of sounds made up of all the vocal creatures of the habitat whose voices are somehow related to one another. Subsequent analysis led to the further notion that the discrimination and complexity of these acoustic patterns could be observed, and that the patterns could also be utilized to determine the physical history of a habitat. How these acoustic features looked in early examples of the study is noted in Figures 3.1 and 3.2.

Figure 3.1 shows a soundscape spectrogram of a secondary growth biophony recorded on Pic Paradis, a mountain located on the French side of St. Martin Island in the Caribbean Sea. The spectrogram graphically illustrates the sound patterns of this sub-tropical habitat, a relatively new-growth environment that had been clear-cut in the 1950s.

The spectrogram provides three pieces of information. From left to right as you look at the image, approximately ten seconds of recorded sounds are depicted. As you scan the spectrogram from bottom to top along the right hand side of the page, you will find an illustration of frequency, beginning with the lowest pitched sound and rising to the highest (indicated by the small numbers to the right of each horizontal line in the spectrogram). The relative amplitude (loudness) of each of the sounds is indicated by the darkness or lightness of the patterns: the darker the pattern, the louder the sound and vice versa. The bandwidths of the insect soundings primarily occupy two niches and are depicted by two thick horizontal lines in the bottom third of the spectrogram. At dawn when this recording was made, two birds filled niches where there was little or no interference by other sounds. A mourning dove (*Zenaida macoura*) sings four times (note the four lines, like dashes, toward the bottom center of the page). The second bird in the sample is a lesser Antilles swift (*Chaetura martinica*). A graphic example of its vocalizations can be seen represented by the five vertical lines that appear on the spectrogram.

The relatively light density of the patterns may indicate that the habitat has not fully recovered from deforestation, even though this was recorded in the spring when vocal density normally is greater. The elaborate acoustic

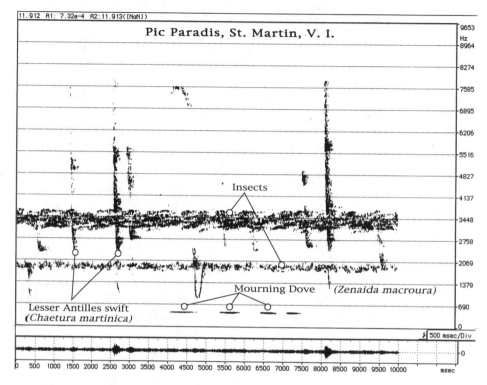

Fig. 3.1 Pic Paradis, St. Martin, V. I., secondary growth biophony spectrogram

fabric that once existed in this habitat is no longer present—partly as a result of deforestation and subsequent habitat loss and disruption, and partly because of the noise from humans who now populate the region.

Figure 3.2 illustrates a more complex tropical biophony that was recorded March 1991 in Borneo. The sound patterns shown in this spectrogram indicate a much healthier and older habitat because of the variety, density, and discrimination of voices. It clearly demonstrates niche differentiation that had very likely been established over a considerable evolutionary period, where a large number of creatures occupy various frequency ranges and times. Two thick horizontal lines across the page show insect vocalizations. Within the white areas, where there is no other vocal energy, the voice patterns of primarily three kinds of birds can be seen. The Asian paradise flycatcher (*Terpsiphone paradisi*) appears two times in three niches simultaneously; the brown barbet (*Calorhamphus fuliginosus*), four times; and the ferruginous babbler (*Trichastoma bicolor*) sounds in a succession of notes. The flycatcher must have taken a very long time to learn a vocalization that fits so neatly within three niches of the audio spectrum. Its exact-

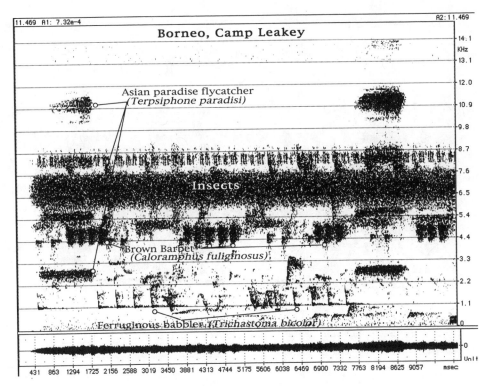

Fig. 3.2 Camp Leakey, Borneo, primary old-growth biophony spectrogram

ing placement of sound may possibly indicate details about the habitat's age and how we might eventually measure it.

When we compare the wilder habitat with the tame one, we begin to see the affect humans have on a sonic environment. Deforestation is only one of many ways that has an impact on our world of sound. The following examples will demonstrate others.

Human Impact on Biophonies

Since 1984 I have been listening to and recording spade foot toads (*Scaphiopus hammondi*) around Mono Lake located beyond Tioga Pass, east of Yosemite National Park. What is marvelous about the toad vocalizations is the way in which one toad begins to sound, then others join in, creating a creature chorus. This is then followed by a synchronicity of sound pulses that absolutely engulfs and hypnotizes the listener. When there are many toads present during a breeding cycle, the aural illusion is created that their chorus is moving in waves around the ponds. A couple of years ago, I was

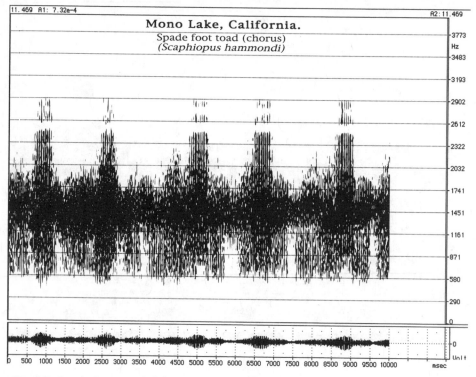

Fig. 3.3 Spade foot toad chorus with synchronicity intact.

able to document a direct correlation between human-induced disturbances to the toads, their defensive response, and related consequences.

The incident involved a low-flying military jet over the Mono Lake basin in April, 1993, one evening while my wife and I were camping and recording. **Figures 3.3–3.6** show what happens. When you are listening in certain habitats, many types of frogs and insects vocalize together so that no one individual stands out among the many. This chorusing creates a protective audio performance that keeps predators from locating any single point from which a sound originates and thus isolating any particular creature. The frog voices emanate from so many places at once that they sound as if they are coming from everywhere. When the coherent patterns are upset by the sound of a jet plane or some other loud disturbance within range of the pond, the special frog choral synchronicity is broken. In an attempt to reestablish the unified rhythm and chorus, individual frogs momentarily stand out. This gives predators, like coyotes or owls, a perfect opportunity to snag a meal. After the jet disappeared, a total of 45 minutes went by before the toads had reestablished their protective chorus. In the

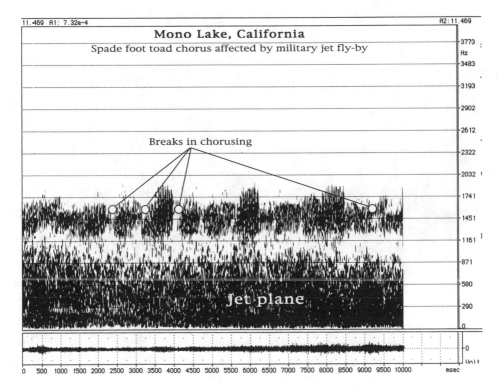

Fig. 3.4 Spade foot toad chorus interrupted by military jet fly-by.

dim light of dusk, we witnessed two coyotes and a great horned owl feeding by the side of the small pond. We discovered that the relatively intense noise produced by a low-flying jet aircraft can cause dramatic changes in the biophony. Certain creatures seem to momentarily lose the life-saving protection of their vocal choruses.

Figure 3.3 demonstrates the protective synchronicity of the toad vocalizations that keeps predators from locating any one organism. This is illustrated by the fact that there are no breaks in the center of the choral example.

Figure 3.4 shows the effect of the fly-over as it occurs. Note the decline in the number of creatures who are vocalizing, as well as visual breaks in synchronicity.

Figure 3.5 shows recordings that were made 20 minutes after the jet flyover; it demonstrates a continued inability on the part of the frogs to resume synchronicity and their recent and continued vulnerability to predators. It was at this point that all vocalizations ceased for some time. It took 45 minutes from the end of the aircraft fly-by before coherent vocalizations resumed (**Figure 3.6**); after that, we saw no more predators in the area.

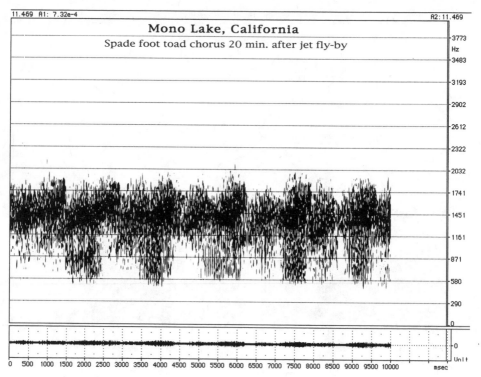

11.469 A1: 7.32e-4

A2:11.469

Mono Lake, California

Spade foot toad chorus 20 min. after jet fly-by

Fig. 3.5 Spade foot toad chorus 20 minutes after jet fly-by illustrating remaining discontinuity.

Figures 3.7–3.9 demonstrate the first noise-related incident we were able to capture on tape and show graphically. The images represent a fly-over that occurred in February, 1990, at a research site called Kilometer 41 in the Amazon north of Manaus. Recording the dawn chorus one morning, my colleague, Ruth Happel, and I, heard a low-flying multi-engine military jet shatter the jungle soundscape.

Figure 3.7 paints a picture of the biophony prior to the presence of the jet. Note the finely delineated and discriminated features of the biophony.

Figure 3.8 shows the soundscape as the jet flies by. The change in creature voice discrimination becomes clear as the jet moves away from the site.

Figure 3.9 shows the continuing impact of the jet noise on the biophony, even when the jet has left the area.

No one knows for certain what types of mechanical noises cause changes in the way wild creatures behave. We do know that noise directly affects *our* experience of wildlife. When I am in the field trying to get a sense of a place, most human noises distract me and often affect the behavior of the creatures I'm there to see or hear. Many visitors to our national parks

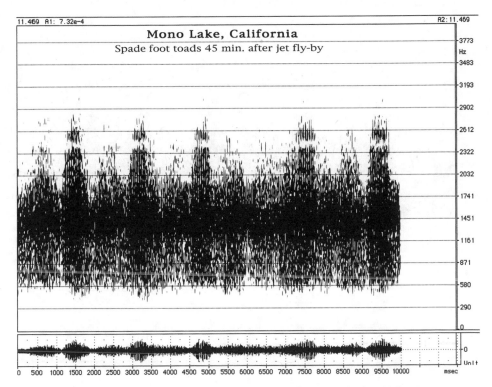

Fig. 3.6 Spade foot toad chorus 45 minutes after fly-by with chorus intact.

have expressed similar concerns. It is not always the loudness of a sound that causes animals to bound over a ridge or to become silent when the presence of an intrusive mechanical device intrudes. Sometimes it's the quality or character of the sound, referred to as *timbre* in music. The fly-over of a Piper Cherokee 140 (a single piston-engine private plane) may have a far different effect on certain creatures than an F-16 jet despite the fact that both are measured at the same level of loudness.

In the late 1970s, humpback whales in Glacier Bay, Alaska, were observed trying to swim away and hide from the noise of cruise boats. The animals ducked behind spits of land or small icebergs that had broken off from glaciers in an effort to find quiet shadow zones. Where once there had been many whales on a regular basis, by the late 1970s when research supported by the National Park Service was under way, there were fewer and fewer whales migrating to the bay. Some researchers cited increased tourist vessel activity as the main cause. Along with variations in krill populations (a tiny shrimp-like creature that is a major ingredient of the humpback diet), and the manner in which certain vessel noise may be amplified by the geo-

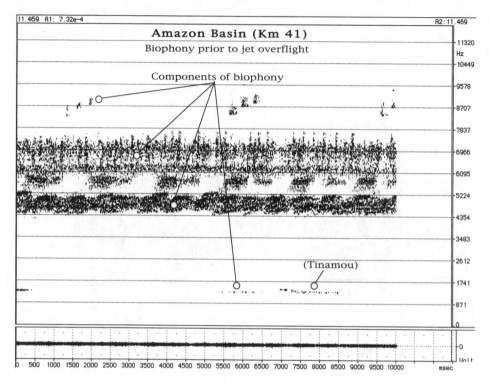

Fig. 3.7 Tropical rainforest biophony intact.

logical features of the bay, human-induced boat noise was considered a likely factor in the falling numbers of humpback whales present in the area.

On the other hand, just south of Glacier Bay's entrance in Icy Strait, and to the east in Frederick Sound, humpback populations thrive during the summer months in spite of vastly greater numbers of boats of all sizes and levels of noise output. While this does not mean they are unaffected by the noise, rarely have the whales been observed swimming away from boats in these areas. Humpbacks feed in these waters during the short Alaskan summer months and must increase their body weight substantially prior to their return migration to Hawaiian waters. To some extent, habituation to the noise is essential to their survival. The stress levels caused by the impact of noise on these whales has not been measured. Nevertheless, nearly every time I have dropped a *hydrophone* (an underwater microphone) in Icy Strait to record the wonderful humpback feeding sounds, I am amazed by the amount of propeller noise generated by commercial and private boats from as far away as eight miles. Yet the whales keep on feeding, playing and vocalizing. Over a period of fifteen years and on as many trips, I have

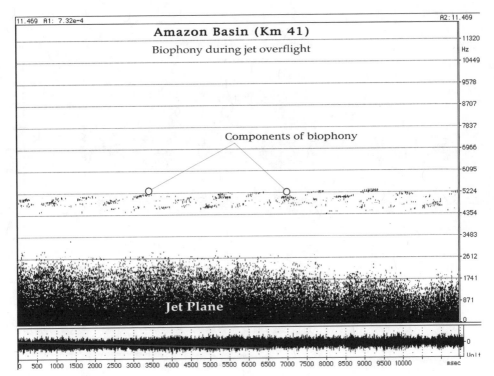

Fig. 3.8 Tropical rainforest biophony interrupted by jet fly-over.

recorded a total of three or four minutes of whale feeding vocalizations (sometimes called "contact" sounds because they seem to lure other whales to the vicinity of the singer). The seductively exuberant sounds of the feeding whales when it was quiet are truly unforgettable.

The natural ambient sounds of special places also change as a result of resource extraction, as occurs frequently in our nation's forest areas. Lincoln Meadow is located a couple of miles east of Yuba Pass on the Sierra Nevada ridge line north of Truckee, California. It was once a pristine edge habitat replete with a wide variety of spring birds, insects and amphibians. It sounded glorious and full of creatures the day I first recorded in 1988. A year later, an area of forest south of the meadow was heavily logged. By 1989, the sound had become hollow and eerie with just a few sapsuckers, distant chipping sparrows, and a mountain quail constituting what was left of the biophony. In June of 2001, I found that even though there were visual signs of recovery in this area, the lack of vocal density and special resonant cohesion between the meadow's creatures was still missing, even though it was spring and normally a time of much vocalizing. I was also

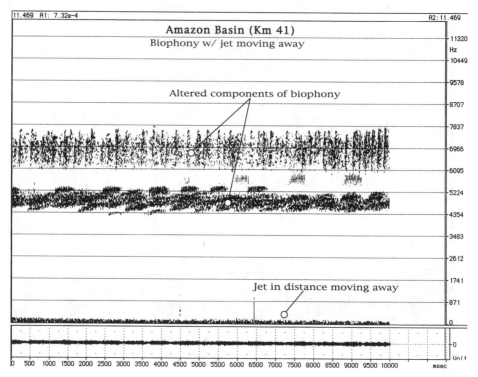

Fig. 3.9 Tropical rainforest biophony still disrupted with jet in distance.

aware of a greater number of airplane fly-overs than previously experienced and there were few *noise-free intervals*. It was still, quiet, and colorless, much like a sick patient in a coma. *(Listen to CD tracks 7 & 8.)*

When researchers consider the effects of human-induced noise as an important factor in natural soundscape loss, the results are notable, particularly in light of the fact that there is no way to accurately measure how animals or habitats may be affected by noise at this time. From my experience and that of many visitors to the national parks, the introduction of noise into natural soundscape heightens the sense of loss because noise diminishes human experience of the wild.[5] During my work in the field, I have noticed a wide variety of changes in creature behavior indicating possible stress when a chain saw revs up or a snowmobile approaches.

The equipment used for voice measurement such as recorders and analysis technology tends to have limitations that creature ears do not and vice versa. And finally, site selection of these studies seems to play a significant role in the manner in which human-induced noise affects living organisms. Human and non-human species respond differently to types, loudness, or combinations of mechanical noises. We are now beginning to understand that many of these sounds introduce distress in animals even though the victims may not *seem* conscious of the effect.

Recently, researchers have measured a fair amount of stress in the Yellowstone elk herds that they believe stems from the introduction of certain kinds of mechanical noise. *(Listen to CD track 16.)* In the spring of 2001, Scott Creel, a biologist at Montana State University, along with his colleagues, reported a link between elevated glucocorticoid enzyme levels in elk and wolves to snowmobile noise in both Yellowstone and Voyageurs parks. These enzymes are related to stress response according to scientists. During the period when snowmobile traffic increased by 25 percent, there was a 28 percent increase in stress levels in wolves. Conversely, within Voyageurs Park, a 37 percent decline in snowmobile traffic between 1998 and 2000 correlated to an exact drop of the same percentage in stress enzyme levels in wolves. Comparable figures were found in elk populations.[6]

Although the study concluded that the stress levels appeared to have no impact on the population dynamics of either the elk or wolves, it did not actually monitor or document any possible aberrant behavioral effects that the animals might have displayed. One could extrapolate that the noise level in Manhattan, Rio de Janiero, Paris, or Jakarta seems to have no affect on human population dynamics either, but that would not quantify or describe the effect that noise has on the physiology and mental state of individuals living in those noisy places.

If we're not very careful, we're likely to end up where we're going

—Henny Youngman

Natural soundscapes cannot be replaced. Nearly one in four of every wild soundscape I have archived in my collection of thousands of habitats, is no longer in existence. No one will ever be able to hear the voice of these habitats again, except on tape. They are forever silenced, fully extinct, or hopelessly altered. Yet, there are rays of hope. We are beginning to understand that pristine natural soundscapes are precious reserves and resources critical to our enjoyment, understanding, and awareness of the natural wild, as well as knowledge of our own history. Without these biophonies, a fundamental piece of the fabric of life is sadly compromised.

In a recent stroke of genius, the National Park Service mandated natural soundscapes as one of our natural resources.[7] This designation allows the park system to guard these natural soundscapes with the same vigilance as they bring to the protection of wildlife, streams, woodlands, and meadows. Along with safekeeping, the park service has developed a strong educational and administrative program to introduce visitors to the enjoyment of natural soundscapes as part of the wild park experience. Soundscapes within the parks are now greatly valued, worth preserving for visitors and creatures, alike. This marvelous program is one everyone can take to heart because of its simplicity and importance. Sadly, the national parks may soon be the only places left in North America where visitors can enjoy the beauty of natural sound unimpeded by noise.

To my mind, nothing heals the spirit and body more completely than the incantations of the wild natural. To re-connect to the potent sonic elixirs found in our remaining natural soundscapes, we must pay attention to the way we once learned to listen, and adopt new, more comprehensive methods of discerning the information arriving at our ears. In other words, we need to think of—and value—natural sound in new ways. Despite our past training, it is exhilarating and revealing to learn to listen to the voices of *whole* habitats as biophonies and to discover what they can tell us as we begin to explore the natural world with more attentive open ears.

1. Marler, Peter and Marten, Kenneth. "Sound Transmission and Its Significance for Animal Vocalizations: I. Temperate Habitats," in *Behavioral Ecology and Sociobiology*, vol. 2, 1977. (Springer-Verlag: Heidelberg, Germany), p. 271–290.

2. Von Uexküll, Jakob. *Umwelt und Innenwelt der Tiere*. (J. Springer: Berlin, 1909.)

3. Johnston, Verna R. *Sierra Nevada: The Naturalist's Companion*. (University of California Press: Berkeley, CA, 1998.)

4. Krause, Bernie. *Into a Wild Sanctuary*. (Heyday Books: Berkeley, CA, 1998.)

5. National Park Service. *Director's Order #47: Soundscape Preservation and Noise Management*, Robert Stanton, Director. (National Park Service, U.S. Government, 1999, revised, December 1, 2000.) For a copy, contact: **http://www.nps.gov/refdesk/DOrders/DOrder47.html**

6. Creel, S.C., Fox, J.E., Hardy, A., Sands, J., Garrott, R.A., and Peterson, R.O. "Human activity and gluccocorticoud stress responses in wild wolves and elks," academic paper in press, 2001. (Montana State University Press: Bozeman, MT.)

7. National Park Service. *Cited above.*

CHAPTER 4

Exploring Soundscapes

Simple Listening Exercises

A wilderness exists in man that refuses to be studied.

—Loren Eiseley

 In the mid-1980s I began taking people on listening and recording *sound safaris* to Alaska, Costa Rica, Australia and Africa in order to introduce them to the world of exhilarating sound. In such locations, you can still experience soundscapes without too much human noise. For several years, I concentrated on the inland and coastal Alaskan habitats around Chichagoff Island, located directly across Icy Strait south of the entrance to Glacier Bay. This area consists of a wide variety of coastal marine and terrestrial habitats. The sub-Arctic coastal Southeast Alaskan area is a transitional temperate region with widely variable conditions. In summer, there are short, five-hour nights; daytime temperatures can sometimes reach into the high 70s or low 80s.

Sound safari participants took part in a number of exercises designed to heighten their awareness of what they heard. As they listened, they were instructed to concentrate on what they could experience with their unaided ears. The group identified habitats, natural occurrences, and creatures by the unique sounds they encountered. (Remember that a soundscape is made up of any combination of components.) Each day a different habitat was explored and its acoustic characteristics were noted during wet weather and dry: the best ways to listen, what was heard, how sound changed with weather or time of day or night, and what creature or non-creature sounds made up the texture of the soundscape. We also explored the best ways to capture these soundscapes on tape. The same general format for defining the components of soundscapes was applied to whatever habitat was encountered: whole biomes, types of interference, non-creature natural sound, invertebrates, birds, mammals, amphibians, reptiles, etc. Just about any type of habitat that came to mind. The most important thing was to identify how two or more of these creature components in a particular biome expressed themselves together as a biophony.

Here's a list of some of the habitats we auditioned in Glacier Bay:

Whole habitats that had representative biophonies:

Muskegs (bogs)
Coastal coniferous forests
Marshes
Lakes
Bays (inner tidal zones)
Riparian zones (fast and slow running water)
Inland coniferous forests
Open marine environments (with whales, seals, birds and airborne voices)
Submarine environments (with fish, whales, crustaceans)
Tide pools
Shorelines

The group also came up with a list of natural habitat sounds that are non-biological in origin:

Non-creature sounds as experienced by representative geophonies:

Rain
Wind (Although not recordable, *per se*, what you actually hear is the effect of wind as it moves across broken reeds, through trees, and other landscapes.)
Fast and slow running streams
Different types of lake, ocean, and inland waterway wave action
Glacier masses moving over land
Glaciers crackling (as ice melts)
Glaciers calving

The group also listed birds and mammals that they heard, including four species of whales, bear, wolves, two types of seals, sea and river otters, sea lions, anemones, barnacles, seventy-four species of birds plus snapping shrimp and fish. Because we were in a northern transitional zone, we heard few insects—mosquitoes excepted. This listing exercise provided a great deal of supportive information about a habitat's health.

When the biophonies of two or more habitats were compared, the Glacier Bay participants were able to identify their location by sound, alone, just as John Muir stated he could locate where he was in the Sierra Nevada mountains through sounds. In one coastal coniferous forest, the members of the group heard and recorded varied thrushes, Swainson's thrushes, ruby-crowned kinglets, robins, marbled murrelets, bald eagles, red-tailed hawks, mourning doves, ospreys, yellow-rumped warblers, the ubiquitous ravens and crows, and an occasional bee or mosquito. In this particular location, we also heard wolves one morning. Non-creature sounds included the effect of wind blowing through the canopy of the forest.

As we moved inland a short distance to a small lake fed by a stream with a tiny waterfall at one point, the biophony immediately changed to include a mix of common loons, robins, American dippers, a great horned owl, a flock of herring gulls, hairy woodpeckers, and swallows. Here, we saw a river otter but it made no sound while we were present. Non-creature sounds at this location differed from the coastal coniferous habitat by the nature of the gently flowing stream, the waterfall in the distance, and the tiny waves lapping on the shore.

We paddled just off-shore and dropped a hydrophone into the water from our kayaks to hear the sounds of humpbacks bubble-netting followed by their "contact" or feeding calls. Bubble-netting is a cooperative feeding behavior that these creatures use to round-up quantities of confused krill. We also heard snapping shrimp, and even harbor seals. Lowering the hydrophone into the tide pool, and then into the tentacles of an anemone (much the way prey might pass by and settle unknowingly into the anemone's mouth), we allowed the creature to envelope the hydrophone in an effort to digest it. Finding nothing of interesting nutritional value, the anemone expelled the hydrophone with a hearty grunt, backed by the bio-phony of barnacles twisting in their shells and tiny rock fish darting from rock to rock in the pool.

⊙)) Try This!

**In order to remember all the details and as a prelude
to your field exercises, always have a piece of paper
and a pencil or pen handy. R. Murray Schafer suggests
the following: jot down five environmental sounds
(not music) that you have heard today and that you
like. Then, name five sounds (not music) that you
didn't like. What makes some sounds pleasing to you
and others not?**

Getting Started Exercises

You can explore soundscapes wherever you live or visit. They exist in
your own backyard, down the block in an open field, the hills behind your
house, and the pond in your city park as well as in undisturbed habitats.
The trick is learning how to explore them. The following soundscape exercises are great fun to do in the field and will help tune your ears.

Let's begin with some activities that will bring all of what you've read
so far together in a more general but active way. No matter where you
decide to try these exercises out, the main objective is to *listen in ways you
may never have done before.*

Find A Quiet Spot: Exercise 1

Find a quiet spot where there is no mechanical or other human noise
and where there are only creature or natural sounds: a stream, a meadow, a
lake, a favorite forest, a mountain, a beach, a marsh or park. You may need
to walk, paddle a canoe or kayak, or ski to get there, but it's worth it. If
you're near a city, you may not find a place that is completely quiet. If you
drive to a seemingly remote spot, remember that others can get there as
well: your location may be noisier than you expect. If you happen to live in
or near a densely populated area, seek out what natural sound recordist,
Gordon Hempton, calls *noise-free intervals* or *NFI*, defined as fifteen
minute periods when there is no mechanical or domestic noise present.

Notice that I've made a distinction between *noise* and natural soundscape. Noise includes any sound that intrudes, covers, blocks, or distorts the
articulation of sounds coming from the natural (as opposed to domesticated) creature world. Turn-of-the-century wit, Ambrose Bierce, once defined
noise as, "The chief product and authenticating sign of civilization."[1] This
has never been more true than today. In the context of this book "noise"
refers to undesirable human-induced or mechanical noises. But domestic

dogs, roosters, cows, or sheep can have the same effect on our experience when we're concentrating on natural soundscapes.

A good time to find noise-free intervals is just before dawn when humans are quietest. It is also a great time to listen because bird vocal density is at its peak. This is true especially in the spring. Give this effort enough time and you'll discover that there is a special aural fabric unique to each particular location. The sounds you hear at dawn, midday, afternoon, dusk, and at night, may define the habitat more clearly and with more detail and clarity than any Ansel Adams photograph. To reach these circles of biophony, don't hesitate to go some distance away from places where human noises tend to be greatest. You'll be rewarded with something sublime nearly every time. Throw away the watch, too, and, for heaven's sake, leave your cell phone and pager at home. Let natural time define itself by waves of creature orchestrations.

Questions to consider as you walk through this exercise: What do you mean by a quiet spot? What do you mean by noise? How does noise affect your appreciation of the wild (or anything, for that matter)? What types of natural sounds within a habitat make you feel good? Relaxed? More fully alive and keenly aware?

Three basic conditions need to be met in order for sound to register in our minds.

- The sounds need to be within a range that human beings are physiologically capable of hearing—roughly 20Hz to 20kHz (one **Hertz** is a unit of frequency in the field of acoustics defined as one cycle per second).

- The sounds need to be loud enough so that we can detect what is being expressed. (This is often noted in **decibels** or dB, where one unit of change relates to the smallest shift the human ear can detect).

- You need good ears that have not been destroyed by high levels of urban or electronically produced noise.

The first two elements take into account much of the creature world, but not all. For instance, many mammals have voices that fit neatly into the range of human hearing, everything from mice and small bats, to large megafauna like elephants and whales. However, there are certain bats and dolphins, and small whales, for example, that humans cannot hear unaided; the voices of these creatures exceed the highest frequencies we can detect. In some cases, a particular creature's vocal range may partially overlap ours, being both higher or lower in *pitch* than what we are able to hear. Elephants and larger whales are included in this category. The highest voiced creature in the mammal world is not a bat, but the blind Ganges dolphin (*Plantanista gangetica*), reputed to have a voice exceeding a frequency of 350kHz—six-and-one-half octaves higher than the highest note on a typical piano. It is thought that one of the large whales possesses the lowest voice—around 4Hz—although it is not known, for certain, which species. The fin whale (*Balaenoptera physalus*) has been heard to vocalize around 15Hz. Elephants, giraffes, and possibly hippos, have special **contact vocalizations** (vocal syntax that draws others to the vicinity of the "singer") that are lower in frequency than what humans can detect without the aid of some technology. In the insect world we can hear maybe 20 to 30 percent of what is represented— only a fraction of the number of species.

Many insects produce signals so high that we cannot detect them, and many have voices too soft to hear. In the avian world, we can hear most of what is represented, although the upper harmonics of some birds well exceed our ability to detect. In the amphibian world, we hear nearly all available sounds (except those voices which are also expressed underwater). Some reptiles, such as crocodiles, produce some of their sounds at a frequency lower than what we can hear, but most can be heard.

There are many voices the unaided ear cannot hear in marine environments such as lakes, ponds, oceans, and swamps. These include, for example, marine insects, fish (near coral reefs, in particular), anemones, large and small whales, shrimp, and barnacles (although at low tide, barnacles exposed on rocks sometimes rotate in their shells and emit a high clicking sound). Our inability to hear well underwater is the result of the ear's design, a model that works best in air. Sounds become muffled when we hear them underwater. Simply put, our ears are not designed to hear well in marine environments. The hydrophone provides a wonderful adaptation that enables us to hear what produces sound there.

If you happen to be in the right habitat where a particular whale sound is loud enough and your boat is single-hulled, you may be able to detect the sounds of humpbacks, bowheads, and killer whales through the hull. Sailors and Eskimo hunters have reported hearing these animal vocalizations in such a manner. In certain forests, some creatures prefer to vocalize at night when dew settles on the ground, or on leaves and branches of trees. Using the forest as a *reverberant* theater or a kind of "echo chamber," nighttime becomes their time to "sing." Particular nocturnal birds, hyenas, baboons, coyotes, and wolves often choose those *reverberant habitats* or special times when the conditions in the environment produce reverberation, in which to vocalize. They even change their voices slightly to accommodate for the echo.

Elk rutting in the fall often use the echoes of the forest to project their voices in order to extend their territory and secure their harems. *(Listen to CD track 16.)* Even killer and humpback whales sometimes vocalize in air, bouncing their voices off nearby cliffs near the shores of Glacier Bay, Alaska, and other environs such as Johnstone Strait, located along the eastern shore of Vancouver Island in Canada. While camping along the northern shore of Chichagoff Island just west of Juneau, my wife and I heard several members of a humpback pod trumpet twenty yards away from where we slept. They chose that spot to rest after long hours of daytime feeding. Some insects, birds, and mammals, like to vocalize when their habitat dries out; after sunrise, when the forest has given up its surface moisture, animal voices don't need to carry so far. Other animals prefer transition periods neither dry or reverberant.

These are a few of the creature sounds you can hear. Now try this exercise to help you refine your listening skills.

Listen Closely: Exercise 2

Once you've found your quiet-spot, listen (preferably with eyes closed) to the ways in which the combinations of creature voices (birds, insects, mammals, amphibians, etc.) define the space. Biophonies may change as you move through sonic territories, and as day and night, seasons, and weather conditions shift through their various cycles. The territories defined by biophonies can be quite small and shaped differently from what you might expect. Each type of habitat—even within the same biome—will provide a number of unique sound signature experiences just like our individual voices. The natural world above and even below the ground, above and below the surface of water, is everywhere alive with vibration.

> *The fish does ... HIP*
> *The bird does...VISS*
> *The marmot does...GNAN*
>
> *I throw myself to the left,*
> *I turn myself to the right,*
> *I act the fish,*
> *Which darts in the water, which darts*
> *Which twists about, which leaps—*
> *All lives, all dances, and all is loud.*

—Gabon Pygmy, Africa

Start a list of creature sounds and try to identify each animal that is vocalizing within the biophony—it's kind of like picking out a specific instrument in a symphonic production and listening to just its notes and rhythms. Cultivate good identification systems to describe what you have experienced. You may have to invent your own descriptive language. While teaching harmony and theory at Yale University in the 1940s, 20th century composer Paul Hindemuth urged his students to "…learn what I have written between these pages, and throw the damned book away."

Some sounds may be very subtle. Learn to listen and discover your totem natural sounds—the ones that especially draw your attention and resonate with something in your soul: these sounds will become key to what you love in those soundscapes, and you will want to return to them again and again.

I've often heard it said that the voice of a creature is dependent on its size. In other words, small creatures have tiny, soft voices. Larger animals are somehow louder. Careful listening will explode this myth. Many small creatures have voices so loud, that if extrapolated pound for pound into larger beasts and heard, we would probably become instantly deaf. The snapping shrimp, for example, is an inch and a half in size. The popping sound it produces underwater is equivalent to the impact noise of a .357 magnum pistol being shot off at your ear. Imagine a snapping shrimp the size of an elephant with a correspondingly loud voice. Other small and very loud creatures include the Pacific tree frog. It's about the size of your thumb nail but its voice registers about 80dBA at ten feet. The hyrax and mynah bird are other examples of loud small creatures. On the other hand, many large creatures have relatively soft voices; the giraffe is an example, except when it is emitting its low frequency sounds, as well as the California gray whale, tapirs, and anteaters.

Listen With a Difference: Exercise 3

There are many ways to listen. You can *cup your hands behind your ears* and slowly rotate your head from side to side. Notice how sounds become louder and more focused as you do this. You'll hear more because your ears just got bigger. You'll begin to hear in the manner of animals who have large ears. The shapes and sizes of their ears help certain creatures locate the direction from which a sound comes.

You can also *make a set of "wolf" ears out of paper* shaped like those of various mammals, such as the bat-eared fox shown here. Shape them so that they can be taped to your own ears or on the stems of eye-glasses. You will get an idea about how other creatures hear and how your own listening ability can be enhanced.

Listen with your eyes closed or blindfolded. Walk toward a stream. See if you can determine how far you are from the water's edge by sound alone. Still blindfolded, face in the direction of a singing bird. Try to tell how near or far away it might be, or, if it moves to another tree, in what direction it has flown.

Questions to consider as you try these exercises: How many different types or families (birds, insects, amphibians, mammals, etc.) of sounds do you hear? Within each group of sounds, how many different species can you identify? Can you distinguish between one habitat and another by the subtle difference in soundscape biophonies, alone? How would you describe the **acoustic textures** that you hear? (For example, *buzz, coo, tweet, whoop, peep, cluck, cackle, hum, hoot, shriek, hiss, gurgle, pulsate, moan, groan, belch, chatter, whisper, rhythmic, scratch, ringing, bellow, pant, breathy, reverberant, dry sounding, etc.*)

Some Tips for Listening to the Creature World

Don't Limit Yourself

Some bioacousticians now believe that every living organism produces an **acoustic signature.** When you are exploring natural soundscapes, don't limit yourself to the larger, most visible species. The very small creatures, nearly microscopic, sing too and have wonderful voices. Several species of ants, insect larvae in pools of water, water boatmen, anemones, and fish all make recognizable and unique sounds. Earthworms create a sound signature as they travel through the soil. Recently, it was discovered that even viruses create sound signatures particular to each type.

Smaller creatures have given me tremendous pleasure because their voices were so surprising. However, many species of bats, insects, and numerous marine creatures, may require the use of some specialized (but not-too-expensive) equipment to enable you to hear them. You'll learn more about this in subsequent chapters.

Best Ways to Hear

When you set out to listen intently, it is often best to be alone. Even then, your attention to the natural soundscapes outside your body will be interrupted by sounds your own body produces. In the field, my stomach grumbles, or I hear myself trying to brush away annoying insects. If you go on a sound safari with another person or with a group, make sure everyone is dedicated to being very still and quiet. No talking. No rustling of clothing. No shuffling of feet, coughing, clearing of throats, or sniffling. You don't have to hold your breath. Just be cool and considerate. Leave all other thoughts behind and concentrate on what you're hearing.

More Getting Started Exercises

Cue in to the Aural Context: Exercise 4

With your ears alone, try to hear the aural context in which creatures vocalize. Beginning with individual birds, insects, or mammals, amphibians, fish, or crustaceans from microscopic to colossal, focus on all the sounds that make up the orchestra. Notice how they blend and the sources from which they come. Be mindful of the subtle differences in the sounds of the flow of streams, creeks, and waterfalls. Tune in to the singing of sand dunes, cells of thunder and rain passing through, wind in the aspens, pines, or maples, the variety of sounds made by the wave action at the seashore.

Most of us hear the sound of crickets, katydids, or other insects and frogs as a cacophony or din of noise. In modern society, this is symptomatic of how we learned to emphasize our sense of sight over other senses. When you listen closely, you begin to discern a wealth of information from sound-producing creatures. Did you know that you can determine the temperature in air by counting the number of chirps made by certain crickets? In the evening, listen to the rhythms they produce. Crickets do this by rubbing their wings together, a method called *stridulation*. One wing has a *scraper*, the other a *file*. The wing containing the scraper rubs against the wing with the file. The subsequent friction produces a sound. Because crickets are cold-blooded, the tempo of the stridulation, or number of pulses in a given period of time, is based on the ambient temperature and its affect on the temperature of their bodies. With the snowy tree cricket (*Oecantus fultoni*) for example, you can count the number of chirp pulses that occur in fifteen seconds, add forty to the number, and arrive at the temperature in Fahrenheit. Other species have different formulae which are similarly easy to determine (i.e., you can add the number of pulses that occur in fifteen seconds to a prescribed number depending on the species). By reversing the

equation you can determine what the formula is for each particular species of cricket in your own backyard or on the trail. Sometimes, during evenings that have cooled quickly, following a very hot day, the crickets within your range of hearing do not have a synchronous stridulation. Where the ground temperature varies because of greater areas of sun or shade, you don't hear the distinctive pulse of the cricket chorus. This is because certain groups of crickets are chirping at a slower rate (where the ground is cooler) while others are chirping at a faster rate (where the ground is warmer). Temperature, of air, water, and earth, is an important component of the aural context.

> *I borrow an allusion from crickets:*
> *their song is useless,*
> *it serves no purpose*
> *this sonorous scraping of wings*
>
> *But without the indecipherable signal*
> *transmitted from one to another*
> *the night would not*
> *(to crickets)*
>   *be night.*

—José Emilio Pacheco

◉)) Try This

You can set up an inexpensive exhibit in your house that features the temperature-telling ability of crickets. It would contain a cricket in a glass jar with an open top, a hidden but accessible thermometer, and a chart with the formula printed on it. Using the sounds of the cricket chirps and the following formula, what is the temperature here? Here's a title for an elementary school science project:
"What Can We Learn from Nature's Voices?"

Other acoustic niches in the *audio spectrum* may be filled with flying or stationary insects, frogs, and birds (like owls or night herons). In undisturbed habitats, listen to them as a *related chorus that blends*, rather than as disparate sounds resulting from the animals competing for a place in the choir. More likely than not, each creature learned its respective part eons ago. Immerse yourself in the creature musical performance.

Compare Related Habitats: Exercise 5

Now that you've had a chance to listen in one spot, move a few hundred feet away and listen to what the natural soundscape tells you about your new location. Notice how the sounds of the insects have subtly changed. Perhaps it's the mix of birds occupying this new territory or, because you moved closer to a pond, you now hear bullfrogs. Explore each area's **acoustic boundaries** to get a sense of the territory's shape as defined by the sounds that emanate from its natural borders. The vegetation and geological features may look the same or be quite different.

As you cross from one zone to another, the creature mix defines the territory with even greater articulation than what you can experience visually. This may be a result of the **territorial syntax** (subtle differences in the phrasing arrangement as expressed in the soundscape) of one or more bird species, groupings of insects, amphibians, mammal mix, or all of the above. Don't think of these territorial shapes as neat square grids with sides measuring 100 yards. In the natural world, territories tend to be more fluid and amoeba-like and often change their borders over the course of each day, night, and season.

Where allowed, don't be afraid to leave the formal trail to discover how a territory is conveyed through the vocalizations of the constituent non-human club. Watch out for poison oak or ivy.

When you complete this exercise out in the wild, review what you've heard. Think about how the sounds all seem to fit together or interact—or, conversely, how they do not. When the vocalizations you hear seem not to relate, these dissonances or conflicts may be a factor of habitat alteration or stress. After a forest has been clear-cut, for example, even when it has been replanted and shows signs of regeneration, it takes some time before vocal creatures find their niche so that they can be heard in concert, once again.

Tips for Field Trips

- Never leave home without taking a few pencils or pens and a notebook with you into the field. (Leave the lap-top computer behind, however—a pencil never runs out of battery power).

- Write down everything you hear in as much detail as you can describe.

- Draw maps (even crude ones) of the boundaries that distinguish one soundscape within a territory from another.

- Describe the sounds you detect and characterize their effect on you. A particular soundscape in the vicinity of the Tetons may include birds like Wilson's warblers, hairy woodpeckers, mountain chickadees, or the chattering of a ground squirrel. It may include a stream in the background or the effect of wind blowing through trees (make a distinction between stream sounds, wind effect, and rain, especially, since they share characteristics of white noise). The sound-scape may also include the drips of water on leaves after a rainstorm has passed, the silence after a snowstorm or in a desert box canyon, something your eye didn't identify as it skittered through a pile of leaves on the ground, the particular way a forest reverberates after a night of rain and how it seems to soak up and attenuate acoustic energy after the sun rises and dries out the leaves, plants, and the earth itself.

In the clearing, where the mind flowers
and the world sprouts up at every side,
listen
for the sound in the bushes
behind the grass.

—Marcia Falk

1. Bierce, Ambrose. *The Devil's Dictionary*. (Dover Publications: Mineola, NY, reprint 1992.)

CHAPTER 5

The Language of Soundscape

New Words for Old Sounds

Songs are thoughts, sung out with the breath when people are moved

by great forces and ordinary speech no longer suffices...it will happen

that the words we need will come of themselves. When the words we

want to use shoot up of themselves—we get a new song.

—Statement by Orpingalik, a Netsilik Eskimo

 Our spoken language contains few references to sound in the natural world. While our language is full of visual descriptions—words that define the physical characteristics of objects we see—it is short on vocabulary to describe what we hear. Even our musical lexicon is replete with terms for sound that are based on the language of sight: "color," "form," "dark," or "light" are a few examples.

From my experience scoring films, most expressions used to compose film music are laced with visual phrases. Directors would frequently say things like, "Try *shaping* the scene this way," "I'm looking for this kind of *color* in the orchestration," "Can you make the orchestration *brighter*?," "Can you make it *darker*?," or "I'm looking for a softer *texture*." Few directors could conceptualize what they wished to hear in aural, musical, or other acoustic terms.

When I needed to describe the combined and related sounds made by creatures in particular locations, I turned to Latin or Greek root words that might easily define certain characteristics of natural sound. *Animal symphony* was way too cumbersome. *Bio* refers to "life" or "of living things." *Phon* refers to the Greek word for "voice." The two elements fit perfectly to form biophony, the voice of living things. Our vocabularies also need to expand in order to more fully describe non-creature and non-human sounds found in various environments — the sounds of water, wind blowing through different types of trees, thunder and rain. When I heard sand dunes singing, the word *geophony* seemed a perfect term to mean the non-creature natural sound: *geo* from the Greek word *gaia*, meaning "earth." Thus, geophony refers to the non-creature sounds of the earth.

Crickets "chirp." So do birds. We need to find precise words to help distinguish the difference. For one thing, the sound-producing mechanism in birds, a syrinx, is different from that of a cricket which scrapes its wings together. Crickets and other insects produce a wide variety of sounds. Many crickets produce a pitched sound (meaning that a distinctive tone is produced) that is both pulsed and rhythmic. Also, sound can be produced by its wings in other ways — sometimes referred to as a *chirr* — a rapid series of amplitude-modulated (loud to soft) tones. A bird's song or call, on the other hand, can be many times more complex with several tones and **overtones** articulated at the same time; but a chirp remains a chirp in our descriptive language.

English uses the word *purr* to describe the contented sound of a domestic cat. Yet, to my ear, this word conveys nothing about the character of the cat's voice. The French word, *ronron*, especially when expressed with the French "r," comes a lot closer to the sound of the happy cats I know and love. However, there is still only one way to articulate a cat's contented voice in each language.

Birders have their own mysterious lexicon. An American robin is described in one book as vocalizing, *cheer-up, cheerily, cheer-up, cheerily*. Have someone read that to you and try to guess what bird it is they're imitating. As we pay more attention to the substance of these voices, and devote some imagination to expanding the language, we will be better equipped to describe the natural wild.

As simple field recording gear has become more popular in the past few years, listeners and recordists are more mindful of the gap between what they experience in the acoustic world and what they can describe. Many times, in our attempt to characterize voices in the wild my colleagues and I resort to esoteric musical terms—music is where our attention to sound has generally been focused. In the latter half of the fifteenth century, a variety of musical expressions that had originated for the most part in Italy, became common in the language of classical composition. From time to time, I fall back on these terms (not all of them Italian in origin) to describe elements of sound. In the following chart, I've listed these musical terms and offered their original definitions along with an example of how they can be applied to bioacoustic field work.

Musical term	Original definition	Bio-acoustic example
Accelerando	*It.* Getting faster	Getting faster as with the wing-beats of a ruffed grouse.
Accent	*L.* Stressing a particular note or beat.	Common in the calls and songs of many birds, frogs, insects, and in the drumming of great apes as they bang on the buttresses of fig trees in their respective forests.
Aeolian	*Gr.* Sound produced by wind.	A whistle-like tone produced when winds blow across or through a medium, such as barbed wire, snags of wood, reeds of different lengths, pine needles, tree leaves, etc. The sound can rise or lower in pitch, depending on the force of the gusts and the medium that is being affected.
Allegro	*It.* Cheerful or a fast tempo.	On the cheery side: think of birdsong on a spring morning.
Andante	*It.* Literally means to walk.	I use this term to describe an insect or frog rhythm that is slow to moderately paced. The way we probably moved our bodies in more ancient times.
Appoggiatura	*It.* Refers to certain notes of a melody moving quickly from one to another either above or below a commonly produced tone.	Frogs and birds sometimes embellish their vocalizations in this manner, as do some species of whales and dolphins.
Arpeggio	*It.* The single notes of a chord played in rapid succession either up or down in pitch; articulated like those played on a harp.	Listen to some humback whale song recordings, or the song of a Swainson's thrush.

Musical term	Original definition	Bio-acoustic example
Bagatelle	*It.* The term first appeared in the early 19th century to denote a short character piece.	In Amazonia, you'll find this type of articulation in the voices of the common potoo and the musician wren. Another creature, the screaming piha, whistles the 5th note in the Western scale, followed by a tonic or main note, then up a 4th before beginning the whole sequence again in another key.
Ballad	*Fr.* A form of music both lyrical and narrative that tells a story.	Humpback and killer whale songs convey a certain lyricism. Gibbon sing duets as well. The biophony of any forest conveys both lyricism and narrative to those who listen for these characteristics,.
Blues	Typically expressed by the "flatting" of the 3rd and 7th notes of a Western musical scale.	In the wild, you can hear this expressive song style in the vocalizations of several species of birds and mammals. For example, the musician wren noted in the *bagatelle* example above.
Cadenza	*It.* A clever improvisation.	To me, that is everything sounding in the natural world, especially when one creature stands out in the biophony.
Choir / Chorus	A group of singers or a grouping of certain instruments in an orchestra.	Creature voices singing in relationship to one another in a given habitat: in other words, *biophony*.
Chord	Three or more notes sounding in intervalic relationships to one another. Of these, there are a limited number of musical types.	In the natural world, this number is exceeded probably by a factor of ten. Listen to gibbon duets in the forests of Borneo and you'll know the origin of a chord.
Composition	The template for a piece of music where all the rules for realization are spelled out in a form like a musical score.	In the natural world, this too is biophony, although the form depends almost entirely on the human ability to perceive it, for instance, the song of the humpwhale, the musician wren, the oropendola, the collective soundscape of the Dzanga-Sanga rainforest, the connected music of the Bayaka. *Then* listen to John Cage.

Musical term	Original definition	Bio-acoustic example
Dissonance	A subjective judgment as to when things don't sound "right."	The residual sound one might hear in a disturbed or damaged habitat such as a clear-cut forest or a dying coral reef.
Drone or *pedal-point*	A constant tone or sound over which all other voices make themselves heard in particular relationships to one another.	The collective sound of insects in a rainforest heard at certain times of the day or night. I have experienced this in the wild in a variety of forms.
Duet	*It.* A performance in two parts.	Often heard among birds, whales, frogs, and gibbons.
Dynamism	Characterized by loud and soft, percussive and non-percussive. Lately noted in Western culture as a kind of musical expression early in the 20th century with composers like Stravinsky.	An expression of nearly all biomes, both marine and terrestrial, that has always been present in the natural world.
Ear training	Learning to make distinctions between one tone and another, between the sounds of one instrument and another.	Becoming familiar again with the sounds that make up biophonies in different environments and by learning to listen.
Falsetto	*It.* In humans, it relates to singing above one's normal range and thought to be unique to people.	Many creatures use a falsetto technique when singing, including humpback whales and cats.
Fermatta	*It.* Pause.	As you approach a pond full of croaking bullfrogs, notice what happens.
Flauto	*It.* Flute-like.	The best example is the song of the *flautista* or musician wren (see the definition of *bagatelle*).
Frog	The hand grip for a violin, cello, or string bass bow.	As Ambrose Bierce suggests: "A creature with edible legs."
Glissando	*It.* A rapid, smooth slide from one pitch to another.	Many birds, whales, and land-based mammals produce vocalizations that exhibit this characteristic. The singing of sand dunes serves as a *geophonic* example.
Gong	*Malay.* A round orchestral percussion instrument usually made of brass and struck with a mallet to produce a deep and complex bell-like sound.	The sound produced biologically by the walrus.

Musical term	Original definition	Bio-acoustic example
Harmonic	Gr. The relationship of one tone or voice to another. Also, the complex series of measurable tones within a single note.	Most birds, insects, and mammals distinguish one group of sound-creators from another (without the use of elaborate laboratory equipment) which helps them to create a harmonic series unique to their own voices needed to establish and defend necessary territories.
Improvisation	(see cadenza)	
Jam	American jazz term for improvisation.	Since creatures taught us to dance and sing, they also taught us to jam long before Louis Armstrong appeared on the scene. The Bayaka pygmies of Africa and the Tuva singers of Tannu Tuva (where Siberia meets Outer Mongolia), demonstrate their ability to jam with the voices of their natural surroundings in complex ways.
Klang-tone or ring modulation	Ger. a tone that results from the instanteous sums and differences of two separate tones played at the same time.	Many creatures have the capacity to sing in this manner without the need for fancy electronic equipment or esoteric definitions: bearded and Weddell seals, for example.
Legato	It. Indicating a smooth transition from tone to tone.	Sometimes whales perform legato sounds, along with other land mammals. I apply the term to birdsong as dawn transitions to daytime, and day to dusk to evening, as expressed in bio-phonies.
Meter	Gr. A measure of beats or accents that establishes time and rhythm in music and poetry.	The natural world expresses itself in broad cycles of day and night, or in seasons. Frogs and crickets establish pulses of time —those lyrical rhythms usually heard at night. Cicadas begin their buzzing definitions of time when the sun momentarily penetrates the canopies of rainforests. Chimps and other forest-dwelling primates pound out distinctive rhythms on the buttresses of fig (ficus) trees.
Ostinato	It. A persistently repeated phrase. In jazz, it is called a riff.	The song of a robin in spring.

Musical term	Original definition	Bio-acoustic example
Poco adagio	*It.* Kind of slow.	The rate at which civilization is moving toward ecological sanity.
Polyphony	*Gr.* Many voices, according to most musical history books. It first appeared in the lexicon in the 9th century but has been a part of non-Western music for at least 30,000 years according to some anthropologists.	A common feature of biophony, non-human creatures have been expressing themselves polyphonically for perhaps 60 million years.
Polyrhythm	*Gr.* Many rhythms expressed at the same time. (See *polyphony* above.)	A common feature of biophony.
Presto	*It.* Quick!	The type of sound you will make as you jump when spotting a rattlesnake. Similar to the rate at which natural soundscape is disappearing.
Rhythm	*Gr.* Regular recurrence of stong and weak beats.	For millions of years, chimps have been pounding out rhythms in the forests of Africa. Crickets and frogs have been dividing the time of night with their wide variety of voices. As I write this, there is a pileated woodpecker outside my window punctuating the moment with hits on the trunk of a hollowed-out tree.
Scat	American term referring to a form of jazz singing made popular by Cab Calloway.	Thrushes commonly express themselves this way. So does the siamang (a type of gibbon), and the baby mountain gorilla.
Timbre	*Fr.* The particular quality of a voice sometimes referred to as color.	In the natural world, it is the unique quality of each individual voice, but also the type of organic soundscape produced in a biome; the aural texture of its biophony.

In his book, *Spell of the Sensuous,* David Abram challenges us to come up with new words to describe aspects of the natural wild.[1] Abram's work is based in large part on the writings of Maurice Merleau-Ponty, a French philosopher who wrote that language, "is the very voice of the trees, the waves and the forests."[2] Excluding the words *loud, soft, explosive,* and others common in the language, most of us quickly reach the limitations of our available vocabulary.

Because of a renewed interest in sounds of the natural world, however, there are signs that our slim vocabulary of description may be changing. Professional listeners, like musicians, composers, poets and theater artists, and field recordists, have been foremost in this search for new language. Joachim-Ernst Berendt in his book, *The Third Ear* (the chapter titled "Landscapes of the Ear") relates a moment he experienced at a lake in Oregon's Cascade Mountains one summer's day:

I am lying on a bed of pine needles by the water…Closer at hand, flies flitting past, dragonflies dancing, mosquitoes circling. Not much for the eyes.

But I hear: silence. It is the silence which I hear first of all. Like a weight that I can grasp. A heavy, smooth weight. My ears feel it as if they were groping fingers. I observe that the weight feels good. I think: You haven't heard such silence for a long time.

I occupy myself with: silence. It is alive. A drop of silence. My ears penetrate it. I am inside it. The drop becomes a universe. A cosmos that begins to resound.

This is the cosmos. First of all, the lake. A rhythmic gurgling. A deep sound— bubbling somewhat—and two higher notes: splashing and sploshing. Triple time, as if the lake were dancing a waltz. This isn't a joyous dance. Rather listless, self-forgetful, leisurely…

The deep gurgling sounds like a tired tom-tom. The two higher notes are wooden, like a ballophone, the West African xylophone. A lake playing tom-tom and ballophone.

Then the first dragonfly makes itself felt. I hear it before I can actually see it. The whirring of its rotating wings. The primordial helicopter. Still more functional than any made by man. More dragonflies follow and I discover: there are many different dragonfly sounds. Higher notes, whirrings fast and slow, and dark dronings. And all possible gradations in between. A scale performed by dragonflies…

…But then—even outdoing those voices—a mosquito like a muted trumpet. Like Miles Davis. Piercing. Striking. A flash of lightning for the ear.

The lower the sun sinks, the more sumptuous the concert…from double-bassoon to piccolo, each instrument glissandos into the next. Duos, trios, quartets, chamber ensembles.

…The water's rhythmic pattern expands. Now I can count up to five before it repeats itself. The gurgling incoming swell approaches to a count of three and recedes to a count of two: a quintuple rhythm not to be found in music. The stress is exactly in the middle: on the third beat. In music five beats to the bar usually involve triple and duple time—or the other way around. First comes the duple and

then the triple time. The water 'Five in a bar' of my lake in Oregon consists of two duple times separated by a sombre thud in between. No resemblance to 'Take Five' by Dave Brubeck and Paul Desmond, the piece which helped so many people [in the West] learn to hear 'Fives.'[3]

Not every professional listener, like Berendt, has been as concerned with translating natural sound into the spoken language. During walks in the woods with his wife, Olivier Messiaen, the *avant-garde* French composer and a fine naturalist, would note in great detail the calls of particular birds he found especially melodic and use them later in his compositions. However, he almost never gave them terms of expression in his native language. Perhaps he felt that the language of music was more precise in its ability to recreate creature expressions in the natural world. Several of his titles demonstrate his naming skills. Despite his exceptional verbal proficiency, Messiaen relied on musical notation as the primary way to express the voices of certain creature life. Although Messiaen attempted to represent some individual creature sounds, he did not create a full vocabulary or musical representation of the wild natural.

How do you capture and replicate the roar of a lion, the stridulation of an ant, the complexities of the song of a Swainson's thrush, a parrot fish, a long-horned sculpin (fish), or the sound signature of earthworms penetrating their soil-world, an entire soundscape of a lake with a mixture of insects, frogs, and loons, all at once by using common musical notation or non-electronic orchestral instruments? We all know that ravens "call," but their range of possible vocalizations is quite extensive; except for the word "call" itself, our language lacks terms for the raven's remarkable vocabulary. The components of natural languages aren't present in the woefully lacking lexicon of words or music.

Composers tend to analyze and itemize the natural world just as scientists do. Where science adheres to models of studies they can replicate, composers incline toward emulating those sounds which represent what is especially musical in their culture. Most are apt to leave out sounds they cannot draft in musical notation or define verbally. While John Cage and Messiaen were both experimental artists, they nevertheless failed to include the sound of a crocodile, a hippo, a wildebeest, or a spade-foot toad in their compositions. What did they find attractive about some voices and not useful about others? These abstractions and fragmentations whereby composers favor some sounds and not others, reflect cultural biases. We decide which expressions coming from the natural world are considered beautiful and appealing and which are not.

R. Murray Schafer is one perfect contemporary example of human connection and harmony between the natural world and music. Fine examples of his work are featured on his recent CD, *Once On a Windy Night*.[4] In the title piece, Schafer takes wind—arguably the most difficult natural sound to replicate—and produces a choral piece that is (pardon the pun) breathtaking and potent. Schafer is among the first to use the term *soundscape*, which, "like landscape, contains many fragments that comprise the whole."[5] Because we're visually oriented, the *seen* elements of a landscape are more easily described (types of trees or vegetation; flat or hilly terrain; green, brown, light, dark, sunny or foggy; animals, no animals, humans, no humans, urban, rural, etc.). These descriptions have become rather common-place in our visual vocabulary and we take them for granted as our way of knowing the world. With a growing interest in the field of natural sound, it is now important to find ways to describe the aural phenomena. Schafer is one artist who is beginning to explore new verbal territory.

When I ask people to describe their favorite natural sound, they invariably choose sound from one of two broad habitat types: either marine or terrestrial. Using no particular words to describe them, they usually mean ocean waves, a stream, waterfalls, or rain, on the one hand, or forests, birds in spring, deserts, and mountains, on the other. The dynamic of natural soundscapes runs the gamut from the softest to loudest sounds heard on the planet, and includes the lowest to highest sounds in the realm of creature life. These ranges contain many subtle yet powerful and infectious forces. Except for the loud-soft range, we not only hear a fraction of what is present, but are further hampered by an imprecise vocabulary. Within the range of sounds we hear is a miraculous abundance of information. The problem is that most of this spectacular data is ignored or remains unprocessed with no language to support it.

From the valley above us, a breeze began to whistle through the aspens, then there arose the sound of a huge pipe organ! Angus [Wilson] walked over to the stream, and with his knife, cut off one of the reeds that stood by the shore. He brought it back, covered one end with his hand, then blew into the other; creating a long, low tone. He pointed to the different length reeds along the stream bed and said, "See what the wind does? That's how we got our music, and that's how you got yours. But you have forgotten." With his knife, he cut holes in the reed and began to play.

Journal entry—Nez Perce Indian Reservation
at Lake Wallowa, Oregon

I was educated to deconstruct whole, healthy systems into their intrinsic parts, from the dissection of frogs and cats to analysis of creature voices that were abstracted from the original habitats. Generally the subjects were presented piece by piece. No vocabulary expressed the holistic manner in which these organisms may be existing in symbiotic relationships to one another. My first courses in bioacoustics in the late 1960s were no different. Bird vocalizations were broken down into species' calls or songs, the limit of their expression. Coyotes or wolves either yipped, barked, or howled. Dolphins clicked or screamed. Humpbacks sang. There was no language for the many types of vocalizations expressed by various species or the ways in which creature voices within a given habitat related to one another.

Every living creature has a *sound signature*—from the smallest microorganism to the largest megafauna. Even vegetation! Once, I was sent to record corn growing in Iowa. I sat in a remote field for two hot August nights with my recorder and mics, swarmed by mosquitoes and fighting off flies. Around midnight, I heard slight popping sounds which grew into lots of popping sounds as the stalks of corn telescoped and grew in length almost perceptibly in the moonlight. The friction caused them to squeak and pop, hence the sound signature of corn growing. Every sound connected in a vibrant interrelationship magnified by the use of my recording gear. I'm still trying to find words to describe the voice of growing corn.

To learn about sound signatures and grow our vocabulary related to natural sound, we need to develop new techniques for hearing. As you have seen, professional "listeners," like musicians and composers, have contributed to this field, but everyone's help is needed. Sound recording has been used to capture natural sounds so that they can be played back over and over again in order to describe and analyze them. Many researchers in this area use sound prints or spectrograms, or vocalization analysis programs to represent individual voices, patterns, and interactions of sounds in various habitats. But, this work doesn't have to remain in the laboratory …and, indeed, it shouldn't. To get you started on sound recording, I'll first introduce you to the history of this fascinating field and then present some information about basic equipment for getting started. The more you hear, the more your sensitivity to animal sound variations and patterns will become. My hope is that this will lead all of us to an expanded vocabulary for characterizing, describing, and communicating about natural soundscapes.

1. Abram, David. *The Spell of the Sensuous*. (Vintage Books/Random House: New York, NY, 1996.)

2. Merleau-Ponty, Maurice. *Signs*. (Northwestern University Press: Evanston, IL, 1964.)

3. Berendt, Joachim-Ernst. *The Third Ear*. (Henry Holt: New York, NY, reprinted 1992.)

4. Schafer, R. Murray. "Once On a Windy Night" (compact disc recording). (Grouse Records: Vancouver, Canada, 2000.)

5. Schafer, R. Murray. *The Tuning of the World*. (Alfred A. Knopf: New York, NY, 1977.)

CHAPTER 6

The Art of Hearing and Recording

How We Hear and How We Can Hear More

God asks nothing of the highest soul but attention.

—Henry David Thoreau

 We can hear a large number of natural sounds with our ears alone. To hear other sounds we need some help. Just as it is impossible to see certain organisms without the aid of a magnifying glass, microscope, or binoculars, some vocal organisms likewise need assistance to be heard. These small sounds are really exciting to explore. For instance, we never could have heard the sounds of the anemones noted in the Alaskan list without the aid of a *hydrophone* (a specially designed microphone for use in marine environments), an **amplifier** (part of our hydrophone system), and a pair of headphones. Check out the songs of whales and ants, and you'll come to know, first hand, just how revealing a microphone and recording system can be.

A Brief History of Sound Recording

The recording of natural sounds began in the late 1870s two days after the first public display of Thomas Edison's wax cylinder recorder. I have long since forgotten where I first heard the story, but myth has it that Edison accidentally captured the sound of an American robin near enough to the "sound horn" of the recorder so that the song left an impression on the wax surface of the rotating spindle. At that moment, the foundation was set for the field of bioacoustics. However, it would take another ninety years until this field of study became fully recognized by academia.

Soon after Edison's wax cylinder was commercialized and became a popular success, Vlademar Poulsen, a Danish scientist, invented his Telegraphone, or wire recorder, in 1898. The first electronically driven system used to record sound, it consisted of a thin wire, fed at a constant rate from one reel to another, past an electronically magnetized record head. In this way, Poulsen laid the groundwork for storage, manipulation and retrieval of large, more minutely detailed samples of recorded information. One of the main problems with this technology was that the wires on which the sound was recorded could become crimped or knotted. When wound on the feed- or take-up reels, the wire tended to become unraveled if it was not under constant tension. Rudimentary editing became possible for the first time although it required cutting the wire and tying knots in the ends which proved to be impractical.

Around the same time, various forms of flat disk recording systems were patented by RCA, Edison, and other companies. These readily available consumer products quickly became popular for recording and storing sound. It wasn't until the late 1920s, after AT&T's invention of the Vitaphone, that a method of capturing and reproducing sound on film, referred to in the industry as *optical sound tracks*, could reproduce aspects of natural sound and became part of a conscious effort to do so. Warner Brothers acquired the rights to the Vitaphone process and approached the Cornell Department of Ornithology, offering to work with the department to record the sounds of birds on film. The company's engineers would demonstrate the technical excellence of their invention and Cornell would identify the creatures and allow Warner Brothers to use the recordings in their film soundtracks.

At the heart of the optical sound technology was the use of light. It consisted of tiny stripes like narrow expanding and contracting vertical bar codes that ran the length of the film strip synchronizing sound to picture. This representation of sound, read by a light projected through the bars of code, projected the pattern variations onto a photo-electric cell in order to create pulses of sound. The first Cornell field recording team of Arthur Allen, Albert Brand, and Peter Paul Kellogg, was formed in the spring of 1935. Brand brought with him a piece of equipment referred to as a *sound mirror*—actually the forerunner of the *parabolic dish*—a device used to capture sound a considerable distance from the microphone. The bulky, awkward, and heavy equipment was loaded onto the back of an old mule-drawn wagon and dragged through marshes in the southeastern United States to a remote location. The technology was so complex that it required two men to operate it. There, the team captured the elusive sound of the last known ivory-billed woodpecker in North America.

When a German group invented the Magnetaphone in the late 1930s, the possibilities of recording extended samples in the field became even more feasible. The engineers who invented this medium, used long, thin quarter-inch strips of paper tape impregnated with fine particles of iron oxide, which, like its wire predecessor, was drawn at a constant speed across an electro-magnetic head, the surface of which was a bit smaller than a human thumbnail. The head delivered a variable magnetic impulse representing an analog of sound that rearranged the particles of oxide into patterns symbolizing the speech or music captured at the input of the system. Once recorded on tape, it could then be easily re-wound, played back and edited. The Germans used it as a surveillance device during World War II. The Ampex Corporation of Palo Alto acquired the technology during the post-war occupation of Europe. Ampex engineers improved both the frequency response and dynamic quality of the audio tape by tweaking the recording electronics. They obtained several patents on the process in 1948 and created a type of reel-to-reel system that has endured for more than fifty years.

Between Edison's day and the late 1960s—except for researchers associated with Cornell and a few marine biologists connected with the Navy's submarine warfare program—very few people were interested in, or committed to, the recording of natural sounds. Most naturalists and biologists chose, instead, to try to capture the essence of the natural world with images on film or canvas and paid almost no attention to the principal thrust of animal communication, their special voices and unique sound signatures. Of those devoted to sound recording, their main effort was the isolation of single creature voices that had been separated from the surrounding aural context. This became the standard academic model. Researchers tended to overlook the sounds of whole habitats as being insignificant or too complex to fully grasp.

Outside of academia, the importance of natural soundscape wasn't even considered as a concept. In fact, it was so overlooked that as recently as the late 1970s, the call of the Australian kookaburra bird could still be heard inserted into the sound effect tracks of both popular and nature films that were obviously shot on location in the Amazon, Costa Rica, or the Everglades. Images of bald eagles in flight would often be accompanied by the screams of a red-tailed hawk. To most of the public, the call of the kookaburra, heard in the early Tarzan and Jane movies made in the 1930s and 40s, came to symbolize the sound of the "jungle." It was not the job of movie directors or media producers to either educate or disappoint us, or so, it seems. In addition to the general lack of interest, stereo sound recording technology until the mid-60s was heavy, awkward, and limited in its recording and reproduction capacities. Insufficient power supplies and the technology's sensitivity to moisture or other extreme conditions made sound recording not terribly reliable in the field.

There was one exception to the ignorance of natural sound that not only startled many in the last century, but also brought attention to a field that was previously unknown. When the first recordings of humpback whales were released in the late 1960s, the overwhelming public response caught record executives completely off guard. These humpback whale "songs," recorded by researchers Roger and Katy Payne, were the first marine examples people had ever heard.[1] The wondrous variety of musical sounds captured on the Payne's commercial record album captivated listeners with the previously unheard underwater world, and piqued interest in the plight of the planet's whale populations. The magic of Payne's recordings also caught my attention and drew me to explore in more detail, the sounds of the wild natural. It also influenced the creative imaginations of serious composers and popular artists like George Crumb, Alan Hovhaness, and Judy Collins.

How We Hear

Our ears receive vibrations that move through the air at a great enough amplitude and within the frequency range we can detect. For those of us blessed with good hearing, our brains process the sound so that we can discriminate between bits of desired information and those that are not. We are also able to determine the directions from which the sounds are coming.

The incoming sound is collected and amplified by the physical shape of the *pinna (Fig. 6.1)*, or outer ear. The pinna collects the sounds and channels

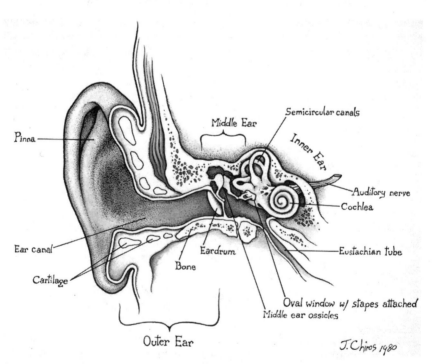

Fig. 6.1 Ear Diagram (courtesy Berger, E. H. [1980]. "EARLog 5—Hearing Protector Performance: How they work and what goes wrong in the real world," E-A-R/Aearo Company, Indianapolis, IN.)

them into the external auditory canal where the acoustic waves are modi-
fied—subtly different from what originally arrived at the outer ear. As the
sound travels through this auditory canal, it is greatly amplified—sometimes by a factor of 2—(particularly in the 2 – 4kHz region). Because the ear
is particularly sensitive in this region of the audio spectrum, loud noises in
this frequency range can be particularly hazardous to your hearing.

The external auditory canal ends at the *tympanic* membrane, which
most refer to as the ear drum. This membrane protects the middle ear from
foreign bodies and vibrates in response to the small changes in air pressure
that happen to reach it. It also transmits those vibrations into the middle ear.
Here there is a series of three small bones commonly called the hammer
(*malleus*), anvil (*incus*), and stirrup (*stapes*).These, in turn, connect to the oval
or round window of the inner ear, the semi-circular canals, leading to a fluid
filled cavity consisting of the cochlea.

In mammals, the length of the cochlea helps to determine the frequency range that we are able to hear. There are numerous tiny hair cells in the
cochlea that are set into motion by the vibrations that have managed to
reach the inner ear. Finally, the sound vibration that has survived the journey through the outer, middle, and inner ear reaches the auditory nerve that
then takes it to the hearing centers of the brain.[2]

Much of the sound that reaches our ears is unwanted information, or
noise, such as traffic, loud noises in a restaurant when we wish to hear what
our companion is saying, background noise in offices with large open
spaces, industrial noises (either indoors or out), and jet planes. In our civilization, our brains have adapted to noise and learned how to filter out
these sounds, while simultaneously retaining and processing what we consider essential. Nevertheless, the noise exists and our brains are doing a lot
of work to eliminate it.

In some professions—for example, musicians in acoustic orchestras—
listening with great discrimination is a feature of everyday life. However,
what many musicians learn to listen to, and for, can be limited by the symphonic structure of the music and the role a particular musician's instrument plays within that system. The best musicians hear a broader range of
sounds. Listening to the voices of the natural world requires similar levels
of hearing discrimination. The layers and textures of sound can extend from
simple to very complex—just like symphonic music. The difference with
natural soundscapes is that they can be many times more expressive and
expansive than the most elegant symphonic music.

The human ear, bound by physiological and neural restrictions, is limited in both its ability to hear very low (*infrasound*) and very high (*ultrasound*) signals. It is also limited in its capacity to hear information that is
extremely soft in volume or very loud (which can cause damage or even
deafness). Our ears are especially sensitive to spatial discrimination. We can
recognize sound coming from overhead, to the right or left of us, in back,
and up and down. We can also recognize the difference between voices.
Some highly specialized humans, ornithologists for example, can distin-

guish the subtle differences in local and regional dialects between birds of the same species. The ear is a wonderfully dynamic tool; there is no known technology capable of replacing its performance characteristics, although some technologies come close.

Getting Started with Simple Sound Recording Equipment

Recording sound is as easy as taking a photograph. When I want to capture some memorable reminder of my journey, instead of a camera I travel with a recorder. With these recordings, I can highlight my journey in the most dramatic way. I can play them for others, use them to evoke memories of the trip, or, in some cases, produce a CD or a performance piece in a large public museum or visitor center where people can enjoy them.

Photos can be taken in a fraction of a second whenever there is available light. Videos can be shot in the time it takes to scan an impressive vista. Unlike taking a photo or shooting video, recording enough sound on tape to establish a sense of place requires more time and patience but is no more difficult. To establish an impression of sound, whether you are listening mindfully or recording, you may need five to fifteen minutes or more to determine what sounds sufficiently define a site or a particular creature whose voice you happen to be enjoying. Recorded sound, like digital photographs or video, gives you instant results. You can immediately play back what you have recorded. This allows you to decide if and when you want to record more. Whether you resolve to collect individual sounds or the soundscapes of entire habitats, once you get your first sound on tape and play it back, I predict you will be hooked and, like me, will want to get back into the field at every opportunity.

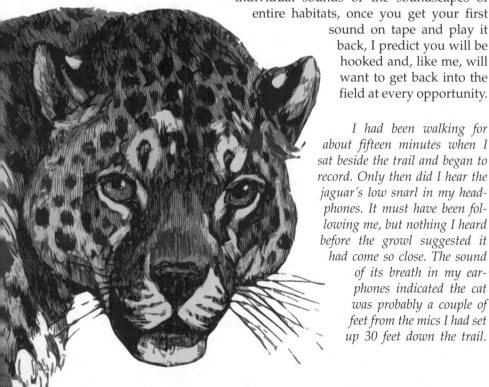

I had been walking for about fifteen minutes when I sat beside the trail and began to record. Only then did I hear the jaguar's low snarl in my headphones. It must have been following me, but nothing I heard before the growl suggested it had come so close. The sound of its breath in my earphones indicated the cat was probably a couple of feet from the mics I had set up 30 feet down the trail.

My heart skipped several beats but I remained still, clutching my recorder with a grip not usually recommended for very sensitive equipment. I managed to record some low growls and breaths indicating it was sniffing the mics, although in the dark, I couldn't see what was happening. An event that lasted no more than a minute seemed to last a couple of hours. I was mesmerized by the power of the animal's voice, breath and the sounds of rumbles in its stomach. Then, as suddenly as it appeared, the cat moved silently off into the forest, leaving only the throbbing pulse of frogs and insects in the night.

Journal entry—Amazon Rainforest, Brazil

Overcoming Techno-fear

If you can take a picture with a still or video camera, if you can use a remote control to turn your TV on and off, if you can warm up coffee in your microwave oven, if you can retrieve email on your computer, if you can start a fire, feed your cat, or scratch your head, you will have no problem recording natural sound. It's that easy.

Despite my own dread of technology, I've found that the use of simple recording equipment and techniques can enhance my experience of the natural wild in ways that landscapes, alone, never can. At first glance, slides and photographs of rainforest vegetation look green and dense, much the same no matter where they were taken. Where there are no creatures represented, these diverse landscapes can be remarkably difficult to tell apart except to the most expert eye. On the other hand, field recordings distinguish these locations through soundscapes as varied and dynamic as the contrast between John Muir and Gale Norton, United States Secretary of the Interior appointed by President George W. Bush in 2001. Nothing is as emblematic of a sense of place as a natural soundscape recording.

The words I will be using to introduce the technology may seem a little strange at first, but the equipment is actually simple to use—remember this is fun! Recording can bring you many pleasurable moments both in the field and when you're back home. You may have questions about how to achieve better sound quality or specifically about your equipment. Many sources are available to guide you. You will find these located in the "Reading and Resources" chapter on page 156. In particular, there is a free on-line help group made up of folks ranging from total neophytes to hard-line professionals eager and willing to answer any questions you may have, everything from currently available equipment to unusual places to record locally, regionally, or even internationally. Called Nature Recordists, you can register free through **naturerecordists@yahoogroups.com** or contact us at **chirp@wildsanctuary.com**. The Nature Sounds Society, based at the Oakland Museum (Oakland, California), offers several introductory field workshops throughout the year at nominal cost to participants. They can be reached through their web site at **http://www.naturesound.org**. In addition, there are a few outfitters and guides that regularly feature sound expeditions to various sites throughout the world. Wild Sanctuary, our company, specializes in sound safaris to Southeast Alaska, Africa, and the Amazon.

A Word about Costs

As with any endeavor involving technology, costs can vary depending on the quality of sound you want to achieve in your new avocation. For as little as $300, you can assemble a credible and easy-to-use basic mini-disc system that you can take into the field to capture hours of decent recordings. If and when you feel ready to commit more time and resources and feel the need to get the best, you can spend upwards of $7,500 for the components to create a truly fine system. Of course, there are many mid-range quality gear combinations in between. Sometimes, the system I choose to use in the field is made up of components that cost less than $1,000. At other times, I bring into the field nearly $6,000 worth of equipment. **Note:** You can compare the quality of a $25,000 binaural mic system with a $700 version on *CD Tracks 13 & 14*: see if you can tell the difference.

Now You're Ready to Record

Now that you have learned how hearing works, and have overcome your fear of the technology (you have, right?), I am going to introduce you to a few easy recording techniques.

First, all recorders have controls that are easy to understand. To record, make sure that your microphone(s) and recorder have fresh batteries. Since all equipment is slightly different, be sure to read the manual for the type of equipment you have purchased. Here are the basic steps for creating your first sound recording:

1. Plug the microphone cable into the "mic input" of your recorder. (Some recorders give you a choice of "line input," as well. If your microphone has a battery in it, try the line input first.) Make sure that your mic is switched "on."

2. Plug your headphones into the hole noted on your machine either by an headphone symbol or noted by text.

3. Load tape or a disc into your recorder.

4. With the headphones on, press and release the "Record" and "Pause" button in sequence. This allows you to monitor what your mic is picking up and the amount of volume coming into the recorder.

5. Set your "record level" with the volume control so that it reads approximately the middle of the scale of the volume meter on your recorder. (This average setting allows you to record a range of louder and

softer sounds. If you anticipate loud sounds—thunder claps or sudden birdsong close to your microphone—set your volume controls at the lower end of the scale so that these sounds will not overload the input, and cause distortion.) Also, set a comfortable level for your headphone monitor (which is a separate control on most machines). Once these are set...

6. Press the "Play" button. You're recording.

Play Back What You've Recorded

1. Press the "Stop" button.
2. Rewind tape to the beginning of the segment (or select the mini-disc cue) you have just recorded.
3. Press the "Play" button and listen to your recording.

⠙ TOOLS FOR ARCHIVING

Whenever I play back a field recording, I hear something I never heard before. I recommend that you take a pair of binoculars into the field to *glass* (see) what you hear. You won't always be successful seeing hidden creatures, particularly in low, or no, light and dense vegetation. Many times you will. To further aid in your explorations of the natural world, there are many excellent field guides to North American birds, mammals, insects, amphibians, and fish. Be sure to have one on hand.

The Field Journal

As part of the recording process and to keep track of what you have recorded, you should maintain a journal of field notes. It not only allows you to re-live and re-visit moments you've cherished, it is also an essential step in the process of becoming a successful natural sound recordist. How many times have you looked at old family pictures that have no identification as to who's who? A field journal will help avoid this problem.

Unfortunately, even though there are a number of graphic insect and fish guidebooks, there are no *audio* insect or fish identification sources (as far as I know). If you are unsure of a particular sound you have on tape, you may want to have your recordings reviewed by a naturalist who is familiar with local fauna. Any information you can provide in your journal will make archiving more exact and potentially more useful. There will be more information related to this subject in Chapter 10.

1. Payne, Roger. "Songs of the Humpback Whales. (Columbia Records: New York, NY, 1970.)

2. Ward, W.D., Royster, L.H., Royster, J.D. "Anatomy and Physiology of the Ear: Normal and Damaged Hearing," chapter 4, in *The Noise Manual*, 5th Edition, ed. by Berger, E.H., et al. (American Industrial Hygiene Association: Fairfax, VA, 2000), pp. 101-106.

CHAPTER 7

Equipment in a Nutshell

Microphones, Headphones, and Recorders

There are many types of recording systems. The simplest consists of an inexpensive battery operated amplifier package (not a recorder) about the size of a deck of cards that can hang around your neck. This little listening device comes with an internal stereo mic system (so you don't have to fool around with extra gear) and only requires the addition of headphones. System 1 *(Fig. 7.1)*, the Amplified Stereo Listener (Cat # 33-1097) costs about $35 plus $10 for the headphones from Radio Shack.

Should you want to record, as well as listen, the Radio Shack stereo amplifier output can be plugged into a recorder so you can use it as your stereo microphone, although it was not particularly designed for that purpose. If you wish to by-pass this step and move right toward listening *and*

Fig. 7.1 Simple stereo amplifier from Radio Shack.

recording, the next level of set-up consists of a recorder, a stereo mic, and headphones. Today's improved equipment has been so well designed that many who have mild technophobia, or who are unfamiliar with this type of gear and think of it as complicated, should reconsider. The professional field system I most frequently use weighs just three and a half pounds and consists of the three elements just mentioned. If you love the wild natural, this is the best field gear investment you'll ever make.

I have been mindful of the fact that wherever equipment is recommended, it needs to be reasonably priced, light, compact, easy to set up, and otherwise simple to use. Three pieces of gear are essential. They are:

1. A microphone (captures the sound).

2. A recorder (receives what the mic picks up and stores the sound on tape or disc).

3. Headphones (allow you to monitor what the mic is picking up and what is being recorded. These are sometimes referred to as "cans").

Microphones (also called *mics* or *input transducers*)

Just as cameras have many different types of lenses used to capture different images, recording often benefits from an assortment of different mics for much the same reason. The language for all lenses, whether they be telephoto, zoom, micro and macro lenses, etc., is common. Mics serve many similar purposes—only they capture individual creature voices and soundscapes instead of portraits or landscapes. Obviously, the simplest systems to understand are those that replicate, as closely as possible, what your ears hear when using headphones or when listening to audio playback using speakers.

Microphone technology is designed to detect and transmit sound to a point of amplification where it can be heard. There are several types of mics, some for recording terrestrial events, others for marine environments. I'll stick to the basics here, meaning simple, commonly used equipment.[1] Each type of mic is designed with a different specialty and pattern. These patterns represent the special ways in which mics receive sound. For instance, *omnidirectional* mics pick up sound from all directions equally *(Fig 7.2)*. *Cardioid* mics feature a kind of heart-shaped pattern (hence the name) ranging from hyper-cardioid (quasi-directional) to cardioid (approaching omnidirectional) *(Fig. 7.3)*. *Shotgun* mics have a very narrow pattern that can pick up individual sounds at some distance from where the mic is pointed (hence the name) while, at the same time, canceling out sounds coming from the side *(Fig. 7.4)*.

Some transducers are *monaural*—meaning a single-source microphone that picks up sound within a single field. Others are *stereo*—consisting of one mic with two pick-up elements or a pair of related mics. They receive sound in a manner that provides a sense of depth, movement through space, and (in some cases) direction. The four patterns noted below represent the ways in which the signal (the sound you wish to record) is gathered from the center of the cross-hairs facing toward the top of the illustration or where a microphone would typically be pointed. Fig. 7.2, the omnidirectional mic, shows how sound is gathered equally in all directions 360 degrees from the center-point of the cross-hairs. In Fig. 7.3, the cardioid, sound is gathered mostly from 180+ degrees from the center-point. The shotgun pattern illustrated in Fig. 7.4, shows how sound is received primarily from where the mic is pointed. The figure-eight patterned mic, which will be discussed later, is shown in Fig. 7.5.

Microphone patterns:

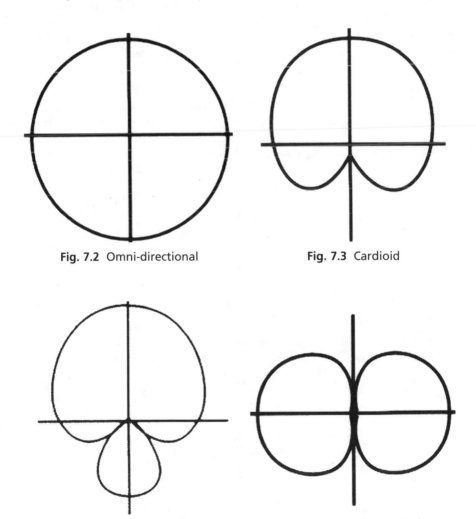

Fig. 7.2 Omni-directional   **Fig. 7.3** Cardioid

Fig. 7.4 Shotgun pattern   **Fig. 7.5** Figure-8 pattern

Monaural

Monaural systems are designed to capture sounds from a single source ranging from individual creature voices separated out from the surrounding habitat to whole habitats. You can use either a shotgun mic which is highly directional, or an omni or cardioid mic. Monaural recording systems are also used to obtain precisely calibrated (tuned) sound pressure level and frequency response measurements in a given location such as during the measurement of jet-aircraft noise levels at urban airports.

Stereo

While other stereo systems exist, only three are considered here because they are the most common and simplest to use. From simple to more complex, they are *XY*, *binaural*, and *M-S*. Each of these systems are comprised mostly of two monaural mics, either of the same type (as with XY or binaural), or different types (M-S) in combination. Sometimes, single tube systems can be found that feature M-S or XY combinations, depending on the manufacturer.

> **XY:** Developed by the British almost seventy years ago, XY systems usually consist of two cardioid (or hyper-cardioid) microphones placed at a ninety-degree angle, nose-to-nose, in relationship to one another *(Fig. 7.6)*. Omni-directional mics may also be used for a stereo effect. Looking at the set-up from the top down, the right mic picks up sound from the left side, where it is aimed. The left mic picks up sound from the right. The sound picked up from the left hand mic usually goes into the right input channel of a recorder. The sound picked up from the right hand mic is usually directed to the left input recorder channel.[2]

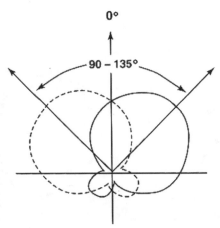

Fig. 7.6 XY microphone pattern
(with a two-capsule combination)

Binaural: Binaural is an expanded stereo technique that promises a spatial recording illusion similar to what we hear. Typically, a model of a human head is used to record—in some cases with a bust of the upper body and head. Small, high quality omnidirectional mic capsules are implanted in each of the ears of the head. (There is even a type where the mics are implanted directly in *your* ears.) Binaural mic techniques are the only ones that tend to capture and preserve all the 3D spatial cues that our ears rely on. In other words, binaural is ultimately resonant with the principles of human psychoacoustics.[3] While, in the past, binaural results fell short of our expectations, even with the use of headphones, new analog and digital playback technologies now under development, promise a more spectacular acoustic result. Usually, these systems are quite expensive.

(As a result of personal correspondence with field recordist Lang Elliott, a more comprehensive understanding of binaural recordings can be found in the Appendix, on page 149.)

⟩⟩ Try this!

A fine binaural result can be accomplished with a relatively inexpensive system. Experiment by tying a piece of string around a tree about the diameter of the distance between your ears. Clip two omnidirectional lavaliere mics (tiny mics that are commonly used by TV newscasters and clipped onto their jackets or ties) opposite each other at the widest point. Mics of this type begin at about $14 each at Radio Shack (a bit noisy and light on sensitivity). Sony ECM 55Bs (or equivalent and not quite as noisy) cost about $410 each. Binaural recordings by this method have fooled even the most hardened tech-freak professionals who swear by the more expensive binaural gear. If you can hold your head still for a long enough time, the lavalieres can even be attached to the stems of your glasses or the rim of your hat. Breathe very quietly and just be sure that you don't rub against the thin cables. As with other head-mounted mics, you'll not only get great binaural sound, but also a stiff neck and a wonderful excuse to visit your chiropractor or acupuncturist. *(Listen to CD Tracks 13 & 14 for binaural recording examples.)*

M-S: The Mid (M) Side (S) system is unlike the others mentioned above in that it combines two *different* types of microphones in one assemblage. Although it furnishes the recordist five optional results from one recording, it is the most complex to use and the least intuitive. This semi-pro and professional-level technology requires some special training to use effectively.

Because of the nature of the M-S system, unless you incorporate special monitoring technology, what you hear coming through your headphones is quite different from what you experience with your ears, alone, or with a normal stereo or binaural setup.[4] Some of the best natural sound recordings are made using just such a system and many recordists feel that the extremely versatile product is worth all the effort although this is a matter a matter of personal taste. Others favor M-S for its flexibility in post-production.

Here's how a typical M-S system is set up: Sometimes one mic (usually the cardioid or hyper-cardioid) is piggy-backed on top of a second figure-eight-patterned mic and both are set in a special *shock-mount* to eliminate vibrations. The top cardioid or hyper-cardioid mic pattern provides some directional pick-up while the bottom figure-eight mic picks up all of the related ambient material in the surrounding habitat *(Fig. 7.7)*. Some current technologies combine the Mid and Side mic elements in a single, cylinder-like unit that automatically encodes the signal into stereo. This allows you to record a stereo result from your recorder while monitoring with headphones thus obviating the need for a pre-amp.[5] The output from the *Mid* mic usually goes into the left input channel of the recorder. The *Side* (figure eight) output goes into the right input channel. Hence the term "M-S."

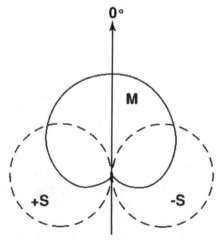

Fig. 7.7 M-S microphone undecoded pattern

You can achieve five possible results with a Mid-Side system because it is so versatile:

- The Mid (M) cardioid or super-cardioid microphone provides some directionality which can be used independently to record individual creature voices.

- The (S) or figure-eight patterned mic records a synchronous ambience that provides more information related to the creature voices picked up by the cardioid mic (M).

- By combining both the M and S signals into a mixing matrix either in the field or the studio you can achieve a robust stereo result that is extremely dynamic when compared to other types of stereo systems.[6]

- After the original recorded data is processed through a M-S matrix to derive stereo, the recordist can obtain the most robust surround result from almost any surround system encoder.

- And finally, assuming there is not much *equalization* or other signal processing in the mix, the recordist/ producer can deconstruct the M-S stereo mix to get an exact duplication of the original M-S recording (using a matrix).

Hydrophones

Hydrophones are designed to record in oceans, lakes or ponds, or any other marine environment *(Fig. 7.8)*. Fully functional models can be made inexpensively for around $30 or purchased completely assembled for

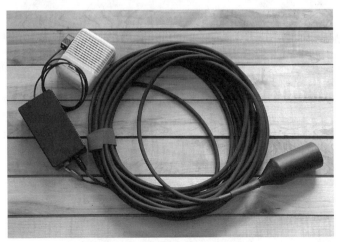

Fig. 7.8 Hydrophone (by Offshore Acoustics, Vancouver, BC)

around $350. More expensive models can cost upward of several thousand dollars but are neither practical or particularly useful unless one is doing exotic research. Because of their excellent low-frequency response, we have been able to record elephant and hippo *infrasound* in air; typical mics don't usually capture sounds in the infrasound ranges produced by these animals. We have buried hydrophones under the sand to record the singing of the dunes and recorded the signatures of earthworms crawling through the soil.

Parabolic dishes

Parabolic dishes are extensions used primarily to focus and capture the sounds of single creatures. Under some circumstances they provide slightly better definition than shotgun mics but are more awkward for field use —especially the large acrylic or plastic models. Usually ranging from about a foot in diameter to several feet, depending on the frequency range of the creature voices one wishes to record, this type of equipment allows very focused sound to be captured from relatively long distances. Size really matters, however. For instance, if a bird has a particular singing range of about 1kHz (one kilo Hertz is described as a rate of sound wave vibration equivalent to 1000 cycles per second) or greater, a dish diameter a bit larger than one foot will do just fine because it can capture a full wave length of sound at that frequency without a problem. However, if the creature voice is a type of mourning dove that vocalizes around 500 Hz., then the dish will have to be at least double in size, about two feet in diameter. If you are heading to Africa to record the low guttural roar of a lion, you will need a dish

Fig. 7.9 Parabolic dish, PRO5W with digital mic from Telinga in Sweden

about thirty-two feet in diameter. (**Note:** by using an omni-directional microphone in the smaller parabolic dish rig, lower frequency voices can be captured without the need for larger diameter dishes.)

The problem with most non-collapsible dedicated parabolic dishes is that they tend to "color" or alter the sound. The same holds true for shotgun mics. Sometimes this is unavoidable if you want an example of a single species among many. But to some extent, all mics color the sound. Luckily, you don't need a giant parabolic dish to record lions, though. Recently, a Swedish company has, with a new space-age plastic, devised a truly clever, collapsible, and foldable dish that expands to about 3 feet in diameter. This device is a fine compromise between shotgun mics and fixed form parabolic dishes and costs about $1,100 from Telinga (*Fig. 7.9*).

Audio Recorders

Used to record, store, and play back sound, there are two types of portable audio recorders: *analog* and *digital*.

Analog recorders can be either cassette or reel-to-reel.[7] While limited in recording quality, standard *audio cassette recorders* provide an inexpensive and perfectly respectable introduction to field recording. They sound better than mini-cassette machines and the results will be less frustrating. The difference between "standard" and "mini" cassettes is size. In the case of analog recording, the larger the recording surface on tape, the better the quality tends to be. Portable standard audio cassette recorders can be purchased from any consumer audio supply store. Prices range from $100 to around $800.[8]

> **Pros:** Standard cassette recorders provide an inexpensive introduction. They can stand a fair amount of abuse.
>
> **Cons:** The most common complaint is the limited quality of their dynamic range and frequency response. This older technology has a fairly high attrition (failure) rate after relatively short usage time. Maintenance is required ("record", "playback" heads and transport mechanism need to be regularly cleaned and de-magnetized). There is no easy way to archive sounds because tape times and location meter readings are inaccurate. These recorders are also expensive to repair.

Digital recorders come in two types: *Digital Audio Tape (DAT)* and *Mini-Disc (MD)* and they range in price from around $200–$15,000+. As of this writing I mostly use and currently recommend the Sony PCM M1 DAT (*Fig. 7.10*). This unit offers a few advantages over other types of systems.[9] The M1 is economical to operate and requires only two AA cell batteries that last about three hours. However, one can get (or build) an outboard rechargeable gel-cell battery that lasts fifteen-plus hours for either machine for around $40–$125 depending where it is purchased. With cost in the $800 range, the deck-of-card-sized M1 is so small and light that it fits easily into

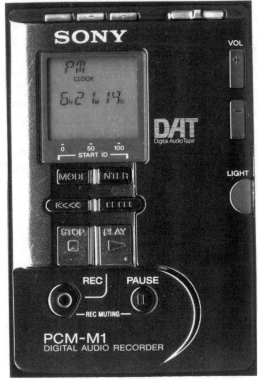

Fig. 7.10 Sony PCM M1

an average-sized pocket. Some field recordists consider the quality of the DAT system to be superior to analog cassettes and mini-discs because of the ways in which mini-discs compress the audio signal. DAT recordings can be transferred directly to computers for editing, analysis, and/or production with no loss in quality—in other words, an exact clone. The recorder takes DAT cassettes designed especially for this technology.

Pros: Medium priced, at around $800, this equipment will last a long time with proper care. (I'm still using Sony DAT machines that are ten years old.) DAT cassettes record 90–120 minutes without having to flip the cassette (as with analog cassette recorders). This allows you to record for long periods of time without running out of tape. It also makes archiving easy because real time and date (the actual time and date you recorded) and tape time (the time from zero to 120 minutes of tape time) are all encoded onto your recording, though this is true only with Sony equipment.

Cons: While they don't require as much maintenance as standard audio cassette machines, the head needs to be cleaned every twenty hours or so of usage. Also, the machine will not operate well under humid or dusty conditions and special attention must be paid to protect it from these problems (a padded zip-lock bag is usually sufficient). No DAT recorder will tolerate being dropped or knocked around much without affecting its calibration or operation. The (female) input/output connectors for the mics and headphones on these smaller machines are 3.5mm stereo mini-jacks (meaning that the holes are small and susceptible to damage). These input jacks require great care so that pressure is not put on them which causes the jacks to loosen. Service charges on these machines are nothing short of scandalous and be forewarned, Sony will take a long time to fix the problem. I have little or no experience with other manufacturers largely because Sony offered more of my required options, but I encourage everyone to check these components out for yourself.

DAT tape needs to stay dry or it will become moldy and will not roll through the transport. Finally, DAT technology is in a transition period and may be ultimately phased out. As of this writing, manufacturers are no longer designing and producing new models and the many brands of DAT recording tape that were available only three or four years ago have been reduced to a relative few.

The new **HHb MDP 500 Portadisc** (mini-disc listed at around $1,545) *(Fig. 7.11)* offers several features useful for field work. While I have not had an opportunity to test it, early reports from colleagues suggest that this technology is definitely worth considering because mini-discs may replace the DAT format. The Portadisc offers a six second *pre-record buffer*.[10] Other, less expensive, consumer model MDs (mini-discs for around $200) with fewer features also exist.

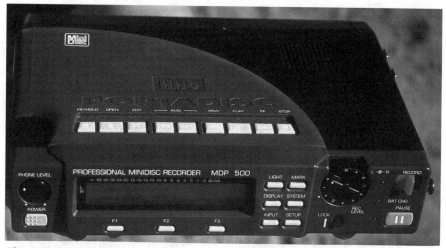

Fig. 7.11 HHb MDP 500 Portadisc   (Photo: Rudy Trubitt)

Pros: This machine is considered extremely rugged according to those who currently use it in the field. It is compatible with both PC and Mac formats for downloading data featuring a Universal Serial Bus (USB), onboard editing, sync recording (synchronous sound-to-film or video), and it comes with many accessories. Also, mini-discs are less susceptible to failure than DAT tape under humid conditions. While DAT tapes tend to sometimes attract mold, the mini-discs are not typically vulnerable to that type of problem.

Cons: Heavier (4.5 lbs) than the M1 (DAT), there isn't enough information to critique the product thoroughly at this point. Those who have used the device report that there were some software and chip problems with earlier versions relating to the time and date coding and an intermittent inability to stop the transport when the machine is in "record" mode. The manufacturer claims to have solved these problems and has sent both replacement software and the necessary chip hardware to end-users to substitute while installing the upgrades in newer models. Reliable field reports from numerous users confirm this claim.

Note: Other Mini-Disc recorders worth considering are the two versions manufactured by Sharp, the MD and the 722 *(Figs. 7.12 & 7.13)* cost between $200 and $300.

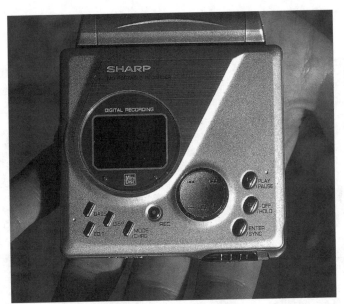

Fig. 7.12 Sharp Mini-disc (no model number)

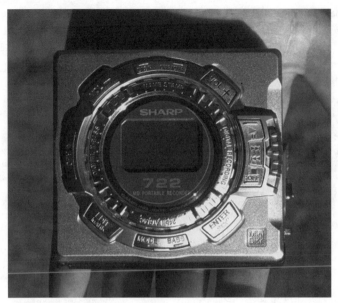

Fig. 7.13 Sharp Mini-disc 722

Headphones (cans)

Headphones come in many types and brands. Stereo headphones that conform tightly to your ears and block outside sound are preferable. There are several brands from which to choose. The Sony MDR 7506 (or equivalents like the Sennheiser eH 1430), as well as several others, cost around $90 a pair and provide everything you need for critical listening and last a very long time.

1. More detailed information can be found in the expert and straightforward book, *The New Stereo Soundbook*, 2nd Edition, by Ron Streicher & F. Alton Everest. (Audio Engineering Associates, Pasadena, CA, 1991.)

2. **Note:** Good quality mic systems of this type can be purchased for as little as $200 to as much as $8,000+. Some come equipped with battery-operated internal pre-amplifiers. Others—usually the more expensive ones—require an outboard pre-amplifier that can cost from $600 to $1,500+.

3. Lang Elliott, personal correspondence; see Appendix on page 149.

4. The signal path leads from the mics to a pre-amplifier that encodes the M-S signal to stereo for monitoring purposes only (through headphones). The output of the pre-amp, still an encoded M-S signal, then goes directly to the input of the recorder where the data is stored on DAT tape or mini-disc. In order to hear the stereo result, the recordist must monitor the signal from the pre-amp and not the recorder headphone output.

5. Sony ECM 957 or 959, for instance.

6. For stereo playback of a M-S signal, the signal output is calculated and derived in the following way: M *plus* S for the left channel, and M *minus* S for the right output channel. The width and depth of the stereo image is continuously variable from mono. This is particularly useful since other stereo configurations (XY and binaural, for instance) can create up to a -3dB signal drop in the phantom center channel whereas the M-S system eliminates this phenomenon (measured in air one dB, or decibel, is an audio term referring to the minimum level of change in amplitude that the human ear can detect). The "phantom center" is an audio engineering expression which refers to the illusion of audio information appearing in between a pair of stereo speakers directly in the center. The sound doesn't *actually* come from the center (there is no speaker there). It just sounds that way when the speakers and mix are balanced properly. With most stereo mic systems, the drop of level in the phantom center occurs because the patterns of the mics fail to cover information coming from that zone at the same level as the side perspectives.

7. Reel-to-reel recorders tend to be quite heavy, expensive to buy and operate, and are otherwise obsolete for field recording.

8. I recommend using Type II (CrO_2) standard audio cassette tape for use in the field. Do not use noise reduction (like Dolby NR which reduces tape hiss) while recording. Ambient noise picked up by the microphone will often exceed most tape hiss you are likely to hear.

9. The Sony D-8 is another small recorder and is slightly less expensive but a bit larger and heavier than the M1. The D-8 is powered by four AA cells that last less than two hours.

10. With DAT recorders, for instance, from the time you hear a bird or mammal you want to record until the time you press the "record" button, several seconds elapse before the transport engages and you actually begin to record. The six-second buffer in the MDP 500, on the other hand, actually captures and stores this sound in a memory chip *before* you hit "record" so you don't lose the beginning of the vocalization you wanted to capture.

CHAPTER 8

Editing and Troubleshooting

The Composition of Recording

To decipher the mystery of soundscapes entirely

would be to decipher a rune.

—K. L. Einreb

 What you collect when you venture out to record sound is actually a composition of sorts. Every choice you make in the field is a type of edit. There is a limited amount of time on recording tape, compact disc, hard drive, DAT or other media you may use to capture sound. Microphones have limited capacities. Recorders, likewise, are limited in their frequency response and abilities to withstand certain environmental conditions. Weather, season, time of day or night, and habitat all play significant roles in shaping the outcome of your recordings. For example, creature density in spring is much greater than in winter. Biophonies at night are very different from those that occur during the daytime. You have more control over these issues than you may think. Here are some pointers to help you master the field skills necessary to become a successful nature sound recordist.

The quality and content of your recording will be a consequence of captured sound as it is processed through all the technology you use to record, mix, and play it back. As it is certainly not the "real thing," it is necessarily an illusion—a partial and transformed representation of what we experience with our ears. The more care you take with each editing choice, the better the result will be.

Recording natural soundscapes is also an abstraction (you get only what the mics pick up which is different from what your ears hear). By the time you listen to a playback of your recording, the sound has been transmitted from your choice of a location with its birds, insects, mammals, and amphibians, to the microphone, down a set of wires, through a number of electronic components to your recorder, to tape, and out, again, to an amplifier and (usually) a pair of headphones or a set of stereo speakers.

All of the choices that you make in this chain of events play a significant role in how the listener will receive or hear the results of your sound recording. To create the best "illusion," you will need to select the optimum combination of elements and equipment. The steps along your decision-making path include not only the habitats and various natural scenarios that you want to explore, and that present themselves to you, but also the various pieces of equipment that are affordable and available to you. Whatever choice you make—whether it has to do with site selection and its impact on finding a recording location, or the area's impact on your equipment, to the actual pieces of equipment you use to record—will be part of a greater editing vision that will affect your outcome. Let's look at some of these factors and how they are related to each other.

Initial Editing Decisions

Select a sound location

Your choice of location will result in a particular creature mix. Be conscious of the impact of extraneous noise (human or geophonic) on your recording. You may or may not want to include this. The important issue is to find a place you like and to record. It can be any type of environment. The exact biome you choose doesn't matter at this point. Within the site you choose, decide which direction to point your mic. Sometimes I choose a direction represented by more creature density. Sometimes less. Also consider the time you wish to begin recording. Remember, there is more creature vocal density around sunrise and just before sunset, but all times of day are represented by some types of sound.

Choose a microphone

In your selection of a microphone, you are making your first edit. In professional recording terms, there is no such thing as a "pure" (usually meaning unedited) recording, so don't waste your time thinking it's possible—even with the fanciest gear. The moment you find an affordable microphone that reproduces the type of sound you like, you have determined your first "edit" and accepted your first compromise (since no mic does all). No matter what the manufacturer claims, every *individual* mic—even the same brand and same type—*sounds slightly different*. The various patterns, frequency response, and sensitivity calibrations all play a determining role in the outcome.

Your choice of microphone will affect the range of what you are able to record depending on its sensitivity, pattern, and whether it is combined with other mics. It will also affect the degree of wind velocity your system will be able to tolerate. To decide what kind of microphone would be best, you need to take into account a balance between your budget and what type of habitat you wish to explore.

Choose systems that are tolerant to harsh conditions

If conditions are dry and windy, choose a mic system that may be less sensitive and features good wind protection. Even the best field mics with super-expensive defenses cannot withstand direct wind gusts of more than six or eight miles per hour without some interference. Omnidirectional mics are less reactive to higher wind blasts. Further relief can be provided by *windscreens*. Windscreens come with almost all mics although some systems are better than others. In a very windy environment, like deserts, where I want to record the effect of wind, I usually use a pair of lavaliere omnidirectional mics setting them low to the ground (if not on the ground) among grasses or bushes where the gusts will not overload the input. This is effective if you can position your mics under a piece of barbed wire that is whistling; changing pitch as the wind velocity increases and decreases.

I choose a system that is less sensitive to high wind (usually most types of omnidirectional mics with a second choice going to the Sennheisers). Each mic capsule is covered with a special type of porous, wind-attenuating

Fig. 8.1 "Fuzzy" cover for wind protection of mics

acoustifoam (a kind of thick foam rubber sleeve that fits over the mic capsule). These are then suspended on a mount that protects the mics from vibration and enclosed by what looks like a plastic (actually nylon) *zeppelin* or blimp-like capsule. This whole setup is usually mounted on a tripod. The zeppelin, in turn, is covered by a "fuzzy" high wind cover *(Fig. 8.1)* that looks a lot like a furry animal puppet created by Jim Henson; this covering diminishes the impact of strong wind gusts even more. Every layer of protection covering a mic input will affect both the stereo imaging and high frequency response to some degree. However, these sound quality losses can be somewhat addressed in post-production, once you return to a facility with the necessary equipment. Some professional field recordists, like Lang Elliott, use a special system comprised of two omni-patterned mics, and also build special shelters to protect the equipment from the strongest gusts. This preparation works sometimes, but if it doesn't, don't despair. Even wind in the most formidable environments dies down at some point. Just pray that the creature sounds you are attempting to record don't stop at the same time.

Rain and humidity present a different set of problems. If either are predicted, you might try using a microphone less prone to failure under those conditions. Mics like the Sennheisers or the Sony ECM 55Bs work especially well—for a while, anyway. Two inexpensive types of mics (around $200 each) will work for short periods in wet or windy environments. These are the Sony ECM 957 or the Audio-Technica AT822. These single-unit stereo mics have two microphone elements enclosed in one cigar-sized cylinder which makes them easy to use in the field. While they tend to be less problematic under humid conditions, they are less sensitive than those noted above. They are also somewhat noisier. They are particularly effective in active habitats with the presence of sufficiently loud creatures. The term used to express this ratio between the signal you wish to record and the electronic noise generated by your microphone system is referred to as *signal-to-noise*. If the proportion of the signal (the sound you wish to record) becomes high enough in relationship to the noise (sound you don't want to record), the noise will not be noticed.

Choose a recorder

You need to feel comfortable with your recorder, whether it is an audio cassette, reel-to-reel tape, DAT, or mini-disc. That includes how it fits into your budget. Some mini-disc recorders fall into the lower end of the price scale. Others reach the upper limits of what you may wish to spend. Many DAT recorders fall into the mid-range. Remember, when you make your investment, that DAT technology may not be available too far into the future.

Troubleshooting

A number of events may occur while recording in the field. Because equipment is subject to failure for any number of reasons, you will want to prepare yourself for those situations. Here are some of the possibilities I have encountered and how the problem was resolved.

What happens when your mics fail? Mics can fail for several reasons: the most common problems are dead batteries in your pre-amp, faulty cable, bad connectors (either at the mic or the recorder), humidity, and particles of dust. Dead batteries are the easiest problem to remedy. A faulty cable can result from a broken wire within the cable (often because it was crimped when stored) or from bad connections at either end of the cable. I usually carry more than one cable with me and replace it, first, to see if this solves the problem. This is much easier than trying to accomplish electronic surgery in the field.

If your mic is sizzling and popping with a kind of static, it may be suffering from excessive humidity. Immediately place it in a well-protected bag of desiccant—a type of silicate grain in small cloth bags that will create a dry climate and eliminate moisture—or in a warm, dry environment. *Don't ever place it on a heater or stove to dry it out!* (Bye, bye expensive mic.)

Once, at a recording site in Kenya, my mics began to sizzle and crackle in my headphones—a sign I immediately recognized as a humidity problem. I extended the legs of the tripod on which the mics were mounted and lit a kerosene lamp under the legs, just to the side and beneath the mics, about 18 inches away. I held my hand comfortably below the mics so I could just *feel* the heat of the flame in order to insure that the rising heat would not damage the mics. A protective metal dish prevented soot from tarnishing the mics. This method dried them out in about half an hour and I was able to continue recording.

Mics can also fail as a result of bad connectors. When they become detached from the contacts they are soldered to, signal transmission fails. A bad connection can also result from defective inputs to the machine that have become loosened. Outputs from the mic are another possible problem source. When this occurs, especially if it is not a connector issue with the cables, it is usually more serious and requires professional help to prevent further damage to your recorder.

While on one of my bioacoustic trips to Southeast Alaska, a novice sound recordist named Merritt found herself some distance down the trail from her tape and battery supplies. A Swainson's thrush had just begun to sing close by. Merritt had forgotten to check the battery that powered her stereo mic and it died after a few minutes. She remembered something brought up during a "what if...?" troubleshooting session. Using her headphones as an impromptu stereo mic system, Merritt was able to capture the thrush's song in a very credible recording. She discovered that headphones can be made to work both ways—as a listening *and* recording device.

What happens when your recorder stops working? First, make certain that your batteries still have some power. If they're working, check to see whether or not humidity caused the failure (which it certainly can in a DAT machine but less likely with mini-disc technologies). Humidity can be caused by condensation on the surface of the DAT tape. After moisture comes in contact with the rotating record head, it can create a drag on the transport mechanism that moves the tape from one spool to another. High humidity (rain or fog outside) can cause malfunctions. So can moving your machine from a cold to warm environment (any change that would cause eye glasses or a windshield to fog up can cause a problem with DAT machines). If this is your problem, most machines will indicate humidity with a representative icon on the control panel.

Check to see that the recorder hasn't somehow accidentally been switched into "Pause" or "Hold" modes. Many smaller machines come equipped with tiny switches that can occasionally snag in clothing or backpack material and get shifted out of position. You can carefully "hot glue" some of the switches in place before going into the field to prevent this from happening; it is possible to dig the hot glue out of the switch with your fingernail or a paper-clip if you find the need to change switch positions. It comes out easily. (*Note: When applying hot glue, be careful not to let the tip of the glue gun come in contact with any plastic parts. They'll probably melt and you'll lose your equipment warranty.*)

 ## Don't Try This!

While working in the Central African Republic, a colleague's DAT cassettes got fungus in them. To restore them, we dismantled the cartridges and unrolled the tapes carefully by hand. The fungus had penetrated the tape shells (cartridges into which the tapes are wound), and glued one layer of tape to the next. DAT tape is thin and delicate. Each time we pulled the layers apart, the tape tore, and each tear required a splice.

If you think brain surgery is a delicate operation, try splicing a digital audio tape and assembling the pieces in sequence so that it still works. On each of a dozen DATs, there were spots of fungus that had to be cleaned; some tapes took fifteen or more hours to restore, yet the recovery of rare Dzanga-Tsonga rainforest recordings was worth the effort.

We immediately made digital copies of our repaired tapes. The message here is: keep your tapes dry and safe by any means you can think of. If you are using a silicate desiccant, make certain that it is still effective. If not, stick the desiccant bags in an oven for a couple of hours at about 175 degrees F. to evaporate the moisture in them and to reactivate the drying properties. Our friend thought his silica gel was still good: it wasn't.

What happens when your headphones stop working? Any wire can break or become unconnected to a plug. If you're concerned, take two pair of cans (headphones) with you.

What happens when it all quits working at the same time? Take a deep breath and enjoy the view. Electronic equipment fails sometimes.

Elements that affect equipment:

- **Insect repellent.** *Never* touch any non-metallic part of your equipment with a repellent that contains *DEET (N.N.diethylmetatoluamide).* It will dissolve anything it contacts. It will liquefy paint and even affect the special qualities of your Gor-Tex®. If mosquitoes tend to think of you as a resource for food, wear latex surgical gloves on your hands. In the summer your hands will sweat, but the plastic elements of your cans and recorder knobs won't melt when touched by fingers that have residual *DEET* on them.

- **Moisture in the recorder.** I once accidentally dropped my new expensive Sony D-10 Pro II DAT recorder into a puddle in a rainforest. For several days I tried to dry it out with blow dryers and other available means. It was the moisture, and not the impact of hitting the ground, that harmed the recorder. Keep your equipment dry! Especially your tape or disc supply. Dry equipment = happy field recordists (plus a clear shot at getting good recordings).

- **Dust and sand.** The transport mechanism of DAT machines is quite sensitive to any foreign element. Keep it clean. This also holds true for mini-disc technology.

Tips to ease your recording life:

- Always check your batteries before you go into the field. Make sure every component that needs batteries has a fresh supply.

- Have a sufficient supply of tape or discs and bring extra stock of whatever you are using. Never underestimate your need.

- Make certain you have the right ancillary equipment (your check-list should include: recorder, right mic for the job, back-up mics, headphones, flashlight, notebook, pen, a bottle of water, rubber gloves, insect repellent, etc.).

- Carry a liberal supply of fresh zip-lock bags (to protect your mics and recorder from moisture and dust).

- Wear comfortable clothing for whatever weather conditions you might encounter.

Things to watch out for:

- Wind and humidity which can affect both the mics and (DAT) recorder. Again, keep your DAT tapes stored in a dry and protected place.

- Mechanical noise, which can include auto traffic, leaf blowers, chain-saws, snowmobiles, aircraft, all-terrain vehicles, trail bikes, boom boxes, etc. All of these make enough noise to carry 20 miles or more if wind and climatic conditions are sufficient.

- Humans who are talking nearby, or moving around and rustling clothing, backpacks, equipment, etc.

- Extraneous sounds in the background that might interefere with what you are trying to record, such as streams or moving water sounds, the effects of wind across trees, grasses, tules, brush, etc.

If you anticipate and prepare for these potential problems, you will have a wonderful time listening and recording in the field. It is possible to minimize almost any difficulty you might otherwise encounter through some foresight and packing the right things for your adventures. Once you understand some of these basics, you are ready for a wider range of sound recording experiments. Read on!

CHAPTER 9

Fun with Listening and Recording

Advanced Exercises

Discover harmony where it is most deeply concealed.

—Heraclitus (c. 500 BCE)

 The following fun activities will let you do some real exploring, stretching the boundaries of your ear's ability to hear and your recording gear's limits on what it can capture on tape. When considering what you might want to listen for or record, always keep in mind three things:

- How your presence might affect any wild organisms and the habitat in which they thrive, because your arrival at any site will most certainly cause many creatures to take notice. Care is important, especially if you wish to get a fine recording.

- Your own safety and that of others traveling with you.

- Federal and state laws are fairly strict regarding close approach and harassment of endangered or threatened species in both marine and terrestrial environments. If you are recording with a commercial product in mind, you may need to obtain a permit to proceed if you decide to record within the boundaries of the National Parks and some state venues.

Many of you are already conscientious about the ramifications of your presence in wild habitats. While listening and recording are fairly harmless endeavors—much more passive than hiking, camping, rock climbing or skiing, you can still leave an impression on the landscape. I'll comment on other effects your presence may or may not have as I introduce the following activities.

The activities noted here are arranged in no particular order. They offer possible adventures based on a number of my own enjoyable field experiences. I encourage you to explore even further, but be mindful of the effects you may have when you enter wild habitats.

Ants *(CD Track 5).* Use a lavaliere mic and lay it on top of an ant hill covering the main entrance. Carpenter, harvester, and several other species of ants, are the most commonly available species to record in North America. Ants usually gather underneath the mic to clear the hole. Some will "sing" (bioacousticians sometimes use the terms "singing" and "vocalizing" in a loose sense to indicate stridulation, the rubbing together of body-parts). Ants are often affected by impediments blocking the entrance holes of their habitats. They gather to remove twigs or any object that impedes their movement to and from their underground nests. Since this activity is natural behavior, I've experienced no problem recording them and observing how they respond under these circumstances. It will cause them no harm. You won't be likely to hear ants with your naked ears so some kind of amplification device like a recorder and at least one lavaliere microphone will be required. Low-cost lavaliere mics can be purchased at Radio Shack. The best one I know of for this type of listening is the Sony ECM55B. Make certain your amplifier or recorder is switched "on."

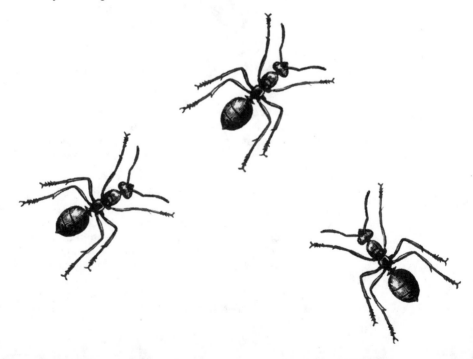

Aquatic creatures. Many species of fresh- and salt-water fish have *acoustic signatures* created by either gnashing their teeth on coral, generating sound with their swim bladders, or even oscillating their caudal fins. Snapping shrimp, those little creatures that create so much static in salt water and brackish coastal marine environments, manufacture sound by forming and snapping bubbles of air in their claws. When many shrimp in a particular habitat are "snapping" at the same time, the result is a static-like noise that sounds something like tuning between stations on an FM radio. In tide pools by the ocean, you can lower a hydrophone into the belly of anemones to hear terrific rustling sounds as they close their tentacles around the hydrophone and try to digest it. It doesn't seem to disturb them; once they've established that the hydrophone is not food, they'll sometimes produce a burp-like noise and spit it out after a few minutes and return to their normal diet. Barnacles, as they twist in their shells, and tiny rockfish that occupy similar tide-pool biomes also produce notable clicking and scraping signatures. Be especially quiet as you approach and leave these aquatic sites.

Singing sand dunes. If you happen to be traveling or living anywhere in the vicinity of the Southwest United States, you are in a perfect location to listen to sand dunes singing. The phenomenon of *singing dunes* has been part of southwestern Native American desert mythology and recounted in Western literature as far back as the turn of the last century in the journals of T. E. Lawrence (Lawrence of Arabia). "Singing" is common at many dune sites located in the desert.

To hear this phenomenon, climb a sand dune (like the Kelso Dunes off the Kelbaker Road, north of Highway 40 between Barstow and Needles, California), then kick sand down the leeward face of the dune and listen to the low moaning and groaning that occurs. If you want to record the effect, bury a hydrophone just under the surface about thirty yards from the top down the leeward slope (the one opposite from where the wind is blowing). Or, use a simple stereo mic and record at the surface. Be sure to protect your recorder from sand by concealing it in Zip-lock bags. Wind usually comes up by late mornings and lasts until early evening. If you are not careful, sand will get into everything. Once it gets into the recorder's mechanism, it is nearly impossible to get it all out—especially in the field.

It's good exercise getting to the top of these 300-or-so foot hills; you can also initiate a sand slide by sliding down the leeward side on your bottom. The dune will burst into a very low frequency song that's really fun to hear and record. It'll be much louder than you expect and will sometimes last for several minutes. Watch the input levels of your recorder if you are recording.

Note: Not all dunes "sing." Of those I know in the Western U. S., only some like Kelso, Sand Mountain (21 miles east of Fallon, Nevada on Highway 50), Crescent Dunes (about 15 miles west of Tonopah, Nevada), Dumont Dunes (60 miles east of Kelso), Big Dune (Amaragosa Valley, south of Beatty, Nevada), and Eureka Dunes (Hanging Rock Rd. out of Bishop, California) are what we consider to be "singers." However, commonly accessible dunes, like those at Stovepipe Wells and the Panamints in Death Valley, do not sing. Researchers are still exploring the reasons for this phenomenon but we have no answers yet.

Fresh water vernal pools or puddles *(CD Track 6)*. After a spring rain pools and puddles are loaded with insect larvae, tadpoles, and waterboatman—many singing! These micro-habitats exist throughout the world. The insect larvae seem to be most active when the angle of the sun is high in a cloudless sky, although there is some activity on most spring and summer days. I haven't yet tried recording in these pools during winter, but there might be activity then, as well. At certain times, the cracking and groaning of melting or forming ice are wonderful natural expressions.

How strange that grass should sing—
Grass is so still a thing…
And strange the swift surprise of snow,—
So soft it falls and slow.

—Gwendolyn B. Bennett

Glacial masses of ice. The sound of glaciers moving over land can be captured by dropping a hydrophone down into a crevasse. What you may hear is the terrifying and powerful low frequency signature of the glacier moving slowly over the ground and, in the process, creating the moraine, or the debris of broken rocks or sand left by the passing icy mass. This sound is typical of glacial movement in many parts of the world. Remember, crevasses are dangerous. The gaps can close at an alarming speed and one can get trapped in such a way that provides few options for escape. I found this out one summer day while recording at the Hubbard Glacier east of Yakutat, Alaska. I narrowly escaped when the mass lurched and closed as I was climbing out of just such a crevasse.

The calving faces of glaciers explode, groan, and grind with terrific force as they break away from the expanse behind them. These instances provide wonderful and dramatic effects truly worth recording. Stay far enough away from the pressure wave caused by the ice mass plunging into the water below and play it safe by keeping your distance. You'll usually get what you need from a quarter mile or so.

After doing some of the easier activities suggested so far, and you become more familiar with recording equipment, try some of these advanced sound safaris.

Create a soundscape following a particular season

Follow a soundscape through a single season or through a number of seasons. Many habitats in the northern hemisphere express themselves acoustically in dynamic ways, especially from early March through June in any given year. Begin recording in a nearby park at dawn provided it is quiet enough. Record samples of your park soundscape once or twice a week every week during the spring for at least 30 minutes—preferably at dawn (or just before and after sunrise). After you collect 10 to 12 weeks worth of half-hour samples, select parts of three or four recordings that best represent your chosen habitat. Align them in chronological order, and play them back to experience the changes in creature density and to hear the resident and transient voices. You can also record samples from one site across all of the seasons.

You might also follow the route of spring as it moves from south to north over parts of the North American continent. In the late 1980s, I did just this, following spring as it moved north sixteen miles a day through the high desert of the west. My colleague was composer, and pianist, Phil Aaberg. We tracked the route many Native American tribes like the Hopi, Navajo, and Utes, had followed during times of their vision quests. We began recording along the "Good Red Road" at the U. S.–Mexican border in Nogales, and moved north to Madera Canyon in southern Arizona. We then traveled past several wilderness areas and the Hopi and Navajo Reservations, into the Four Corners region of Utah, slickrock country in the

Escalante, Goblin Valley, Capitol Reef, the Gray's Lake Refuge area in Idaho, the Teton Basin along the western slope of the Tetons, north into Montana and through the Gallatin and Lewis & Clark National Forests, into the Sweetgrass Hills and on to the Canadian border. Our plan was to stick as closely as possible to the 111 meridian in order to record the sounds of spring as the season moved north through high desert country.

All along the route we camped and recorded samples of high desert environments. This path across the open expanses of the American west is full of acoustic wonders ranging from dead quiet, unmeasurable by even the most sensitive scientific instruments, to violent torrents of rain and flash floods that erupt during sudden afternoon thunderstorms. In a place so quiet that sensory deprivation can drive a person nuts within a few minutes, we were startled one evening by the chirp of a lone cricket hiding somewhere in a nearby seam of slickrock *(CD Track 17)*. In other areas, where dense vegetation would seem to offer a range of creature voices, there were absolutely none. In some places where there were a few recordable wild creatures, their voices would be interrupted by the sounds of cows, sheep, roosters or dogs heard from a mile or more away. Jet planes occasionally broke the spell of these fragile wild voices. Sometimes our batteries died or our tape ran out at critical moments. Keeping a sense of humor, patience, and a positive outlook brought us the successful recordings we sought.

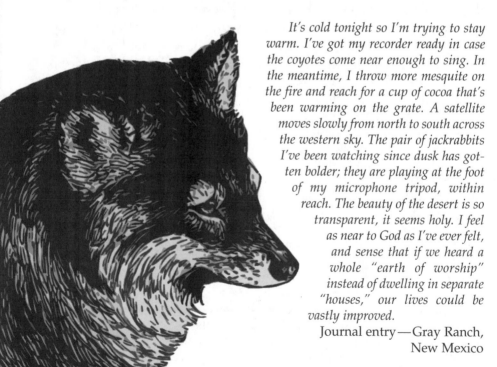

It's cold tonight so I'm trying to stay warm. I've got my recorder ready in case the coyotes come near enough to sing. In the meantime, I throw more mesquite on the fire and reach for a cup of cocoa that's been warming on the grate. A satellite moves slowly from north to south across the western sky. The pair of jackrabbits I've been watching since dusk has gotten bolder; they are playing at the foot of my microphone tripod, within reach. The beauty of the desert is so transparent, it seems holy. I feel as near to God as I've ever felt, and sense that if we heard a whole "earth of worship" instead of dwelling in separate "houses," our lives could be vastly improved.

Journal entry—Gray Ranch, New Mexico

Create your own story or journey

Follow the sun from east to west. It is fascinating to record dawns or evenings from different parts of the country during a particular season or over several. If you have the time and the inclination to travel to remote places, sample events at the equator traveling the globe in either direction. Pick a well-known river like the Hudson, the Mississippi, the Columbia, the Rhine (Germany), the Seine (France) or the Volga (Russia) and follow it from source to delta. Walk the crest of the Appalachians in the Eastern United States, or the Pacific Crest Trail in the Sierra Nevada Mountains in California, or the Rubys in Eastern Nevada. Follow and record the route of Lewis and Clark's journey from St. Louis to the Pacific. Follow the 1,700 mile journey of Chief Joseph of the Nez Perce tribe where he and many other chiefs and related groups out-ran and out-fought five American armies for four months in 1877. Their flight began in northeastern Oregon, over the Lolo Pass in Idaho, south through the Bitterroot Valley, across Yellowstone, ending at the Bear Paw Battlefield in Montana near the Canadian border. These sound safaris offer limitless possibilities, exciting vacations, and a connection to the land you will never forget.

Follow water from its source

Trace the route of a major river from its source in the mountains to the ocean, recording and archiving each habitat along the way.[1] First, find a nearby river and locate its origin. Then map out locations to record along its route. It may end up at another river, a fresh water lake, or the ocean. It will certainly take you through many different habitats and places you may not visit otherwise. This will include variations of water flow, creature voice density, and human sounds, all of which are part of the soundscape.

Species-specific recordings

Birdsong is the most commonly recorded natural sound. These sounds have been traditionally considered "sexy" by collectors from the very beginning of recording technology. Plan to collect a variety of local or regional bird, mammal, amphibian and insect sounds. You will discover that the song dialects of common species differ from place to place and this, alone, may be of interest.

Some field recordists use playback systems in the field that consist of a cassette or CD featuring the requisite bird or mammal sound recording, an amplifier, and one or two speakers attempting to lure birds or mammals close to microphones to either sing, do calls, or just be photographed. Unless you understand the limits of this type of activity, I would urge anyone to work with a trained field biologist who can read the body and vocal language of the creatures you are attempting to entice. (The ethical consideration is based on how strongly you feel it is right or necessary to engage in this type of interaction. If you have to ask the question in the first place, it probably isn't.) Generally, baiting of any type is an activity I steer clear of. I would encourage you to push beyond the common collections, though, and venture into new territory, like tracking the sounds of different insect species, amphibians or mammals in your region. Some of these are very hard to get and require great patience and a lot of planning. It may even require special equipment.

Aside from the usual parabolic and shotgun systems used for capturing the sounds of single species, recordist and naturalist, Lang Elliott, captures birds and frogs, collecting them individually while, at the same time, providing a sense of the habitat within which his target species can be found. He does this with a special mic system he has assembled that is referred to as a SASS (Stereo Ambient Sampling System) technique and that provides a result similar to binaural.[2] This type of species-specific highlight recording with background ambience can also be effectively done using the M-S system described earlier with the inclusion of a hyper-cardioid mic (more directional) replacing a regular cardioid Mid mic component.

1. Wild Sanctuary was once asked to create a sound sculpture that began at the headwaters of the Colorado River in the Rocky Mountains and followed the river all the way to the Gulf of California. You can hear this sound sculpture in Denver's new aquarium.

2. A mono-compatible, near-coincident array of microphones designed to give highly localized stereo imaging for loudspeaker reproduction. (See *The New Stereo Soundbook*, 2nd Edition, R. Streicher & F. A. Everest, Audio Engineering Assoc.: Pasadena, CA, 1998.)

CHAPTER 10

After You've Recorded

Archiving and Creating Projects

We have been constructed out of libraries existing long before

those of man. One is the book containing the genetic code of organisms

present and past. The second is a long list of musical scores

from which all nature sings.

—Inspired by the writings of Loren Eiseley

 You've ventured out into the field. You've listened. You've recorded some interesting bio-phonies or captured some single creature voices. Now, you sit in the midst of piles of tape or stacks of mini-disc boxes. There are probably some great sounds recorded among them, but how will you ever be able to find just those? As with photography and the inevitable pile of good and useless snapshots, some recordings can be weeded out while others are worth keeping; and you will want to arrange the "keepers" into a pleasing and evocative expression of your journeys into the field.

Without first organizing what you have, your recordings may get lost or mixed up, especially if you have a large number of samples. Once these are systematically organized, the field recording excerpts can be "conformed" (arranged, compiled, or mixed) into a finished CD presentation. This chapter will guide you in a step-by-step process that will help you organize your sound recordings piece-by-piece and take you into the process of conforming your recordings into finished pieces.

How to Archive Your Recordings

Too many great libraries have been lost to floods, hurricanes, fire, wars, earthquakes, nasty divorces and separations, not to mention sabotage, vandalism, carelessness, or the concessions made to the digital age. If only the scribes of the great library of Alexandria, destroyed by fire around 1600 years ago, had backed up and stored their data, all of the problems of the 21st century might have been solved by now! So, while you have a chance, follow some simple procedures to archive your precious sound recordings.

Back up your data

The first thing you will want to do when you get back to your home after a field trip is to make a back up of anything you have recorded You need to make a duplicate copy by either burning it onto a CD, another minidisc, or DAT. This is comparable to backing up data on your computer from the hard drive on to disks or other media in order to avoid being caught by a "crash" where all of your records are lost—I don't trust the medium (or myself) well enough to feel confident that something won't get lost, altered, or destroyed. My grandmother used to call this nagging element of doubt "healthy skepticism."

Keep the original recordings and the copies in different locations (and that means it is a good idea to keep one set at a completely different site, not just a different room).

Recorded data is not considered safe or archived unless it is copied and stored properly, so you want to be sure your tapes or discs are kept in a cool, dry place where exposure to sun, heat, moisture, or other debilitating factors can be prevented. It's a good idea to make a note to yourself about where you have stored each version along with the general contents or subject matter.

Make a log

After you have your back-up copy stored safely, make a list of what you've heard, and when and where you heard it. After any field recording session, I return home and replay the tape, referring to my field journal, as I take careful notes related to events that occur in each cue. You can enter the information directly into your computer, but try to do it while the field experience is still fresh in your mind.

Your list of important information should include the date, times of day or night, and other useful "locator" information. You'll want to write down any creature voices or physical phenomena whose sounds you have captured. Note any sounds or vocalizations that you recognize and describe the ones you do not. Here's where "the language of sound" becomes challenging as you try to characterize the specific voices that you have heard. You can rely on your field notes to help you pinpoint the creature voices that you know. If you don't know all of the creature voices at this stage, register that as well. Later, you can return and reevaluate the material and you will find your notations about the time of day, location, activity of creatures you spotted, and biome useful in developing a more thorough accounting of the soundscape you recorded. You may even want, at some point, to play your recording for someone who can identify birdsong or animal vocalization, in order to flesh out your written archives, but first, get everything you can down in your list. The more information you can provide with your first listing, the easier it will be to refine it down the road. You'll also want to make some reference to the quality of the recording. Quality reference is useful information if you are considering the creation of a CD or sound-scape program for others to hear. It saves a lot of time when you want to choose from the best material available.

Here's a short list of information to include on your log, and how it might look in a database format. You can customize the format to your own interests or needs:

Cue:	The identification of the sequentially recorded segment on a DAT tape or mini-disc. This cue, or segment, is noted on all DAT and mini-disc recordings every time you record a new piece of information.
Location:	The identification of the site where the recording was made.
Date:	The date the recording was made.
Time:	The real time of day or night when the recording was made. (I use military hours because the reference is less confusing and universally understood.)
D-time:	The actual time on the DAT tape measured from the zero time at the beginning. (I split this into hours:minutes:seconds.)
Sp. ID:	Species identification, if known.
Quality & Notes:	Quality is measured as follows: 5 = excellent, 1 = poor. Notes refer to special conditions you may want to refer to when archiving or finding material for special purposes.

A SAMPLE SOUND RECORDING LOG

Cue	Location	Date	Time	D-time	Sp. ID	Quality & Notes
1.	Yukon Delta Alaska	6/2/94	0450	00:00:00	R. ptarmigan	(5) No wind. Close. Light birdsong in bckgrd.
2.	(same as #1)		0632	00:23:30	Arctic loons	(4) nesting pair
3.	Askinuk Mtns	6/3/94	2235	01:04:15	Arctic fox	(4) Lite wind. mid-field. Solo.

Getting the most from your log

You can obtain all kinds of useful information from your recordings. Once you have a more complete idea of the creatures you have recorded, you may wish to create an even more detailed index. This might include GPS (global positioning) or GIS (geographic instrument systems) locations, weather, phase of the moon, country, types of equipment used, etc. This type of information can be particularly useful as the number of recordings in your collection increases. It is a feature that can be combined with your photo and video library, as well, referenced in relationship to what you may have shot on film or video tape.

The final stage in good record-keeping is to create a template that allows you easy access to your data. A thorough record will indicate the provenance of the recording and provide any cross-referenced information that you anticipate as being useful. Formats can change depending on your goals and requirements. For instance, new formats will likely include mini-disc recording technologies as part of the equation once we begin to utilize them in the field and they become practical and reliable for professional field applications. The sample below illustrates the information one might want to incorporate in a database program. There are many programs available that can be adapted to suit your needs. As with any equipment choice, select software with which you are comfortable; it doesn't have to be complex to be useful.

I use several categories of information for my archive format, broken down into five broad classes:

1. Tape library information
2. Biological data related to the recording
3. Location of the recording
4. Date and weather
5. Recording technology information

Creating a tape library

If you are considering the possibility of doing serious research or creating an archive of sounds that will be utilized commercially, more extensive detail about your recordings will be needed. Museums and film directors have become very sensitive to the credibility of the soundscapes they use and want to be certain that the information provided by the field recordist is completely reliable in every regard. In addition to the simple field notations mentioned above, you may wish to expand your range of related data and cross-reference what you have.

As you create more and more recordings, you will quickly discover the benefit of being able to find particular sound samples without a fuss. That's when this refined archiving system serves its purpose. Here are some categories to include in a sound library:

RECORDING DESCRIPTION DATA

Library ID#: Ascribes a sequential numbering system to your sound recordings and gives you immediate access to the highest number of cumulative DAT, mini-discs, or analog tapes found in your library. For instance, the first tape I recorded was #1; the most recent was #78,156.

Title: This is useful if it is a completed (or anticipated) project. For instance, all of the DAT tapes related to my CD titled *Amazon Days/Amazon Nights* reference that title. Sometimes, I just reference the location of the recording in this category based on the particular site.

DAT: The highest number of consecutive DATs in the library.

MD: This is the mini-disc number.

PNO: This refers to the program (or cue) number on the DAT or mini-disc.

Duration: Length of cut (cue or program).

Analog tape: This is distinguished from a DAT tape and should have a separate numbering system. If you begin to do your fieldwork with standard audio cassette recordings, you will need to retain this category, when and if you switch to digital.)

N/R: This refers only to analog recording noise reduction systems like Dolby SR.

Absolute Time Start/End: This refers to the beginning and ending times of each cue on the tape.

CD #: This would be the highest consecutive number of your CD backup recordings in the library.

CD Track #: Each uninterrupted recorded sequence in a series.

BIOLOGICAL DATA

Category of creature(s): bird, mammal, fish, amphibian, etc.

Biome: as in Arctic, boreal, desert, sub-tropical, tropical, etc.

Aquatic Habitat: fresh or salt-water environments, also streams, lakes, ponds, marshes, swamps, etc.

Terrestrial Habitat: as in land-based environments

Common Name: as in crow, robin, elephant, killer whale, etc.

Species Name: as in *Orcinus orca*

Sex:	M, F, hermaphrodite, etc. (if known)
# of Individuals:	(if known)
Vox type:	actual vocalization, stridulation, aversionl, contact, feeding, echolocation, lek, song, etc.
Field notes:	special information related to the recording (not represented in other parts of the template)

LOCATION DATA

Country:	
State/Province:	
Site:	
GPS:	actual Global Positioning System location
Altitude:	(elevation)

DATE AND WEATHER DATA

Recording Date:	
Season:	
Weather:	
Climate:	
Temperature:	

RECORDING DATA

Recorder:	If you have a number of machines of the same type, refer to both type and serial number.
Microphones:	Same as recorder info.
Mic. Pattern:	Cardioid, hyper-cardioid, omni, shotgun, parabolic, etc.
Source Distance:	Distance of vocal creature(s) from microphone.
Recordist:	Person responsible for the recording.
Quality:	This rating is important because it will help save time during production or finding a cue you wish to hear again. A standard way to rate the quality of your cuts is using one through five, with one representing poor; two, uneven; three, fair; four, good; and five, excellent. However, this is up to you; just try to create a system that works and then stick with it.
Type:	Two-track, four-track, mono, master, copy, production copy, etc.

Library ID# [1751] Title [Zimbabwe 3 (1996)]

DAT # [408] PNO [2] Duration [10:09]

Analog Tape # [ ] N/R [ ] Absolute Time Start [1:00]

CD # [452] CD Cut # [6] Absolute Time End [11:09]

BIOLOGICAL DATA:

Category [Ambience] Biome [Subtropical]

Aquatic Habitat [ ] Terrestrial Habitat [Riparian dry]

Common name [Ambience (morn), Species [?,
Rattling cisticola, Cistacola chiniana,
Kurrichane thrush, Turdus libonyanus,
Green-spotted dove, Turtur chalcospilos,
Bleating warbler, ?,
Chinspot batis , Batis molitor,
Black-backed puffback shrike, Dryoscopus cubla,
Scimitar-bill wood hoopoe, Thnopomastus cyanomelas,]

Sex [Unknown] # of Individuals [ ]
Vox Type [Dawn]

Field Notes [Morning amb. Rattling cisticola (warble), Kurrichane thrush (8:08:00), Green-spotted dove (8:08:23), Bleating warbler (8:08:50), Chinspot battis (8:09:20), Buffback shrike (8:16:00), Red-billed wood hoopoe (8:16:20), Bru bru (alarm) (8:16:40). Some pops in channels. Recording in what's called the Fringe Mapani edge / scrub.]

LOCATION:

Country [Zimbabwe] State/Province [ ]

Site [Gonorezu]

Altitude [820m] GPS [ ]

DATE AND WEATHER:

Recording Date [9/28/96] Local Time [0712]

Season [Spring] Climate [Cyclic Wet-Dry]

Weather [Clear] Temperature [ ]

Sunrise/Moonrise [ ] Moon Phase [ ]

RECORDING DATA:

Recorder [D-7] Microphones [Sony ECM-55 (Lav)]

Mic Pattern [Omni stereo] Source Distance [Near field]

Recordist [Krause, B.] Quality [Very Good]

Type [Field Recording]

[To Index] © Wild Sanctuary 1997

Fig. 10.1 Typical archive page layout (formatted in FileMaker Pro)

Your recording will never sound like an actual habitat when you listen with unaided ears. Every time you listen to a playback of a place you have recorded, you'll hear it differently and discover something new. Your mood may have changed, your level of attention, your body chemistry, and other life experiences will all affect how you will experience each listening of your recorded soundscapes. These recordings keep teaching us how to listen. Because they are so engaging, I listen to them often and, as a result, keep adding information to my archive log sheets. When I played a recording of a southeast Alaska soundscape for a colleague recently, he noted a particular bird that I had not previously recognized and by calling my attention to its lovely song, I added the information to the archive log for that recording.

Keep your information simple and accessible with clear, cross-referenced notation. Finally, if you are doing a great deal of recording, be sure to keep your archive up-to-date so you don't have to wade through piles of material at any one time.

Creating Projects with Your Sound Recordings

You will soon discover that a natural sound recording is worth a thousand pictures. No words or photographs can convey the power or dynamic of a place with more clarity. While slides or videos may vibrate with light, and film or video with the sensation of movement, soundscapes engage us at a different sensory level of resonant truth and kinesthetically take you back to the places you have visited or lived. A still picture of a black bear pawing my microphone may put a nervous smile on your face. Listening to the recording of the bear sniffing, growling, and then biting the same mic, will make the hair on the back of your neck stand up. So, once you have recorded, once you have archived, what's next for enjoying and using your precious library of sounds?

Unless you are recording urban soundscapes, your recording will consist of two types: species-specific (individual) creatures, or the more contextual perspectives of biophonies. At some point, you may want to produce an audio CD for your family or friends. There are now easy-to-use technologies designed just for this purpose; they are usually digital and consist of software and hardware that can accommodate editing and mixing of more than one stereo pair of tracks. Available in both PC and Mac platforms, the products range in price from around $100 to over five figures. With reasonably priced software like *PEAK* or *ProTools Free* for MacIntosh computer platforms and *CoolEdit*, *Sound Forge*, and/or *ProTools Free* for PCs, one can do simple editing, signal processing (equalizing), and mixing of the different recordings into nearly professional-sounding programs. Visit your nearest pro- or semi-pro audio dealer for the latest updates and tools. The following describes any of several forms of production you may wish to try.

Assemble (or conform) your sound collection into finished programs

To record and minimally archive material, all you need is a strong interest in being outdoors in the wild natural and the ability to hear. Plug in two cables, and push a few buttons (*Play*, *Record*, *Stop*, and *Rewind*). With the time you spend and the recordings you make, you can create a variety of projects and products to enjoy yourself or give to others. From making CDs of species-specific recordings in which you feature the voices of a number of creatures within one animal category, to creating a natural sound sculpture, or a mixed recording of natural sounds and music or other sounds, the creative projects are endless. Here are some ideas you might want to pursue. Most of them are fairly simple; some require an investment in special equipment.

Species-specific: This method of recording single creature voices is used to highlight individual species. By isolating species from their aural context, you can get a closer sense of their vocalizations and learn about their respective acoustic characteristics. This form of production (bird-by-bird, frog-by-frog, insect-by-insect, etc.), lets you present the creatures' distinctive voices, including alarm calls, territorial vocalizations, songs, contact calls, feeding calls, and mating calls. It is particularly useful as an introduction to creating a sound recording "product" and is quite easy to do if you have the right production equipment and software.

First, familiarize yourself with the editing software. While I've never created species-specific programming for a commercial CD, I have done so for museum installations. However, a fine example of this type of recording technique, is Lang Elliott's recent book/CD titled *Music of the Birds: A Celebration of Bird Song*.[1] Elliott describes the calls and songs of the birds and amphibians in informative and loving detail. There are also other CD recordings of species-specific sounds available on the market, most of them for birds, some for frogs.

Biophony: Recorded habitats provide a much broader soundscape context than the more traditional species-specific recordings. For that and other reasons, I prefer a recording of creature symphonies or biophonies. It is more expressive of the natural world as a whole, and you can create dynamic mixes much more evocative of a sense of place than with more traditional species-specific approaches. From recordings made over the course of one or more days from a single site, create a simple mix that consists of a dawn ambience, a midday ambience and a dusk ambience. Take care to blend (or *cross-fade*) the beginnings of each segment so they make smooth transitions.

Use your recordings as sound sculptures

Sound sculptures can be created for many different types of media. This includes film, television or radio broadcast, audio CDs, multi-media performances, and public space exhibits, among others. Recorded sound was first introduced to interpretative displays in public spaces (museums, aquaria, zoos, etc.) in the early 1950s, after the introduction of inexpensive monaural reel-to-reel tape recorders. Mostly, these early designs featured a single sound source and speaker system that typically performed one of two types of programs: push-a-button-hear-a-sound, or repeated extended linear sound loops that represented a snippet of a given habitat or even a single creature voice. Public space sound sculpture installations are audio media performances prepared for venues where public education or entertainment is the main point of the exhibit. With a tropical rainforest CD, four speakers, a surround amplifier, and a CD player—$1,200 worth of mid-line sound equipment—a dramatically forceful portrayal of biodiversity, depth, and impact can be created. Even more powerful non-redundant public space delivery systems provide features that can change audio levels as crowd density varies, or can identify all of the featured creatures in real time as they are heard, and are interactive with visitors.

Sound sculptures apply the medium of sound in much the same way as a sculptor thinks of giving shape to clay, wood, or metal. You can create sound sculptures to enjoy in your home or to give as gifts. They can be soothing and inspiring to listen to and there are a number of occasions when a well-recorded and interesting sound sculpture will be a welcome and surprising gift for a friend or member of the family.

In creating a sound sculpture, be aware of both negative (silence and softer sound) and positive (distinctive and louder sound) space to define and articulate the basic recorded material. You can also mix (arrange) elements you've recorded to form cohesive works of art for either CDs, production, public spaces, or web sites set up for streaming audio. These media are not the only ones for which sound sculptures might be created. The field is wide open with an ever wider variety of locations and environments that might benefit from a prepared soundscape. It is only as limited as our imaginations.

Once you get a sound track you like, experiment with different ways to play it back. First, try a monaural system—one that plays only one track from one speaker. Then try a stereo system—one with a stereo (two-channel) amplifier and two speakers or stereo headphones—and listen to the difference. Then listen to playback with an average surround system (if your audio tracks have been encoded with surround data). With each progressively higher level of technology you choose, the performances become correspondingly more powerful and engaging (assuming that you are working with decent recording equipment and have recorded good quality material to begin with). At the highest level, you can have your program operate interactively with your audience.

With an inexpensive computer, and inexpensive passive infrared sensors (PIRs) like those you can buy at Radio Shack, you can set your system up with two CD players so that if, for instance, you are playing the ambient sound of a tropical rainforest and one of your audience members walks by the sensor, it will trigger the CD to play the sound of a jaguar, or the sound of birds being flushed out of the under-story into flight. Your listeners will be captivated, informed, and delighted with the realism of the experience.

For interpretative purposes, the raw field recordings you use for these mixes need to be noise-free, well-recorded (preferably in some stereo format), mixed and documented. Long, fifteen-to-twenty minute uninterrupted recorded segments are especially favored for smooth, seamless-sounding results.

Combine human music with natural sound

For centuries, composers have been emulating aspects of the natural world and putting them into their musical scores, from Beethoven's 6th symphony, the "Pastoral" to the tone poems of Liszt, to Vaughan Williams' "The Lark Ascending," to Olivier Messiaen and others. Musicians and composers have tried to represent everything from the four seasons to birdsong, to wind, and to the sea. Once you have a natural soundscape on tape, you might want to try to mix it with other kinds of sound—like pre-recorded music—to see how it works. You may even wish to *sample* a particular bird, whale, or primate voice and use it as the basis for a piece of music you wish to compose.

Create a web site audio program

If you have the software, you can create other products from your recordings. These might include customized audio CDs, CD-ROMs, DVDs or web site *streaming audio* (continuous long samples of sound perhaps with some video or other imaging) that provides ongoing, informative and entertaining views of the natural soundscape experiences you wish to share.

If you're into creating web sites with audio, the most common currently available download formats are MP3™ and Flash™. There are others such as RealAudio™, Shockwave™ Audio, Liquid Audio™, QuickTime™, and MPEG and Java Audio. Another source for MP3 information can be found at **www.MP3handbook.com**, where you can download the *MP3 and Internet Audio Handbook*. (**Note:** To access the latest software and hardware technologies, contact your local semi-professional or professional audio dealer.)

The web is a marvelous medium for sharing your sound recordings and audio information about a favorite natural site. If done right, you can give visitors an aural preview of what they might find during an actual visit to your favorite place—assuming you want to share that information. Or, you can create audio postcards to send to friends and family. Printed out, these might take the shape of an envelope the size of a CD (5" square) with a graphic and an audio CD of a favorite location you have recorded.

It is easy to get hooked and involved in making field recordings. Although analysis, archiving, and production take more time, all of these additional activities will help you learn more about the environments, creatures, and biomes that you have recorded. You will want to experiment and may need to dedicate resources such as money and time, not to mention incredible patience to realize your objectives. Often, I will sit for thirty hours in one spot without moving in order to capture the sound of a single creature. What you're waiting for may or may not happen. Something else may surprise you and you will have been prepared to record it. You may not even know what you have captured on tape or CD until you get back home.

It's all a process of discovering the voice of the natural world. Sound recording is one stage in the process of acquiring greater knowledge about the habitats you record. Once you have a good working comprehension of your equipment, the greater will be your success, and further discoveries will open their doors to you.

1. Elliott, Lang. *Music of the Birds: A Celebration of Bird Song*, book and compact disc recording. (NatureSound Studio: New York, NY, 1999.)

CHAPTER 11

Recording Production Techniques

Developing Expertise

My youthful isolation resulted in love of quiet retreats...

[I felt like] the animal who in general seeks hideouts and silence

because noise increasingly... represents the first aspects

of possible danger and violence.

—Loren Eiseley

 Art generally involves a process of transformation when raw "materials" are turned into something new, whether one is describing the process of transformation of wet clay to pottery, or paint and canvas to paintings, or letters in an alphabet to poetry or novels, and individual waves of sound becoming symphonies. The art of recording natural sound is no different. The composer and author W. A. Mathieu once wrote: "When you put a frame around something, it's a picture. Any moment lifted out of time is a photograph."[1] Of course, Mathieu was speaking generally about art.

Once the pressure waves of natural sound reach a microphone that has been selectively positioned, and then transformed in the recording process to bits of tape, a change has occurred and a frame of time has been placed around the recording. What appears within that "frame" will be anything from exciting to boring. Therefore, the sound recordist has a great deal to do with the quality and interest of the final recorded product and is, in essence, functioning with the insight and abilities of an artist.

Here are some of the elements of a well-represented natural sound recording:

It includes a sense of depth. This is created by a robust stereo imaging (derived from XY, binaural, SASS, or M-S techniques). If recorded well at the outset, it will provide the listener, sittting between a decently balanced pair of speakers, a perspective of space as suggested by sound movement on both the right- and left-hand sides, as well as from the near-field (front) to the far-field (rear) which allows for an illusion of depth.

Care is taken to give "presence" to the voices in the recording. These voices must be crisp and clearly distinguishable one from another; they should also be free from distortion and encompass the kind of detail you might expect when looking at the feathers of a bird under a magnifying glass.

The artist (assumed to be both the field recordist and producer) has built content into the mix. This usually means that the artist has included creatures loud and soft or which move through the acoustic space in the piece. There is sufficient drama introduced by these particular dynamics. All habitats contain these aspects of expression. Because a CD is not the real world, but an abstraction or representation, any choice the artist makes that goes into the "frame" becomes part of a mix.

The artist has left his or her unique stamp on the recording. We each hear the sounds of the natural world differently. The ways in which each artist chooses to express his or her mix is unique. When you listen to natural sound recordings, listen for the recordist's sound signature.

The recordist/producer's name and some information about where and how it was recorded are offered. An additional benefit would be the location of the original recordings and identifications of the creatures featured on the CD. This information is always helpful to the curious listener.

Finally, no horsey-manure claims like "pure" or "un-edited." Every recording contains edits or choices of what goes and what stays. Every natural sound recording, like other recordings, is a mix —whether or not the recordist and/or producer had a hand in the necessary ingredients.

Ultimately, it is up to you to hold our attention with your work. The best natural sound art demonstrates an adept metamorphosis of the source medium—the field recording—as it becomes a new, finished work (CD or other media). Some sound recordists do this better than others because they thoroughly understand the processes of their craft and push its limits. It is the inherent responsibility of the artist to produce stellar transformational work. In that regard, it is either greater or lesser art.

Developing Production Expertise

Natural sound recordings that were published and sold in the late 1960s sounded dull to me. Although marketed and packaged well, for the most part, these products were not only poorly recorded in the field, but badly edited back in the studio. They had all the earmarks of producers and mixers who didn't know how to listen very well and who didn't know how to capture the essence of what was present in the natural world. Nevertheless, there was a thirst on the part of the general public for natural sound recordings, inspired, oddly enough, by the voyage to the moon where we viewed the earth as a whole biological unit for the first time, and burgeoning environmental movements that drew attention to overpopulation, habitat loss, pollution and other issues affecting the planet. Roger Payne's recording of the songs of the humpback whale was an overnight sensation and remains in print after three decades. There clearly is a need and desire for solidly recorded nature soundscapes and now, more than ever, there are a few good CD soundscapes appearing on the market.

The prime goal of any recording is the creation of an *illusion* that conveys an honest sense of place. This may seem like a contradiction, but remember that the recording will never be the same as what you hear in the living soundscape. Sometimes you can accomplish an honest sense of place by simply setting up a mic in a spot and letting the tape roll. Often, however, the final result will need some editing, and, dare I say it, mixing. In either circumstance, serious editing has taken place.

First, the recordist had selected a particular mic(s), chosen for its appealing or unique sound qualities. Then, he or she chose a tape recorder. A time of day and a locale were decided. Finally, the recordist culled through the selection of material from the field data and made selections of what would be used in the final CD. A dozen or so editing choices comprise any recorded soundscape. Therefore, any CD that it is hyped as being "pure" or promoted by a producer who considers himself or herself to be a "purist" simply ain't so. The voices of the natural world are at once eloquently sensual and lyrical and any recording is, at its very best, a successful abstraction. Look for quality work that expresses the dynamic power of the illusion.

Judging a Quality CD

When selecting CD examples for reference, ask yourself this question: How well does the CD command your attention? When artists are passionate about their work, they ensure that great care is taken at every step to deliver to the kind of expectations that result when people have to shell out money, spend time, and buy equipment to play the CD. The recordist is obligated to use the best representative recordings in their library.

Doing It Yourself

As with any other art form, you develop an aesthetic sense about the art of recording by judging what you hear as differentiated from what you wish to hear, and what you want others to hear of your efforts. To get to this point, you will need to ask yourself some questions:

- How do you feel about what you have on tape?
- Do you like the illusion of space you are creating?
- Do you like the dynamics of the piece?
- Does it hold your attention as it moves from moment to moment? Are some sections too long or short? Too loud or soft?
- Does it convey the sense of the place you have recorded in your mind's ear—a sense of turf that distinguishes it from all others?

By asking these questions, you will learn to record biophonies of locales that best represent your experience. You will find ways to reduce your recordings to the time limits of a CD in a way that both frames your aural document and maintains its cohesiveness. In my "Sound Decisions" example, you can read how my own recording decision-making process functions in the field, in this case in Alaska.

Sound Decisions—An Alaskan Case Study

It took me fifteen years of field recording to gather enough material to issue a CD representative of Southeast Alaska. While I probably had enough material on tape to produce a CD at almost any point, I could have faked the soundscape by adding licensed recordings of others to mix into the soundscape as many producers have done. However, I knew that the continuity of the soundscape would have suffered. Whale blows from earlier recordings contained some engine noise from boats in the vicinity. The Swainson's thrushes and bald eagles didn't sound quite right due to background noise from nearby streams. The grizzlies and wolves sounded far away and indistinct. Sometimes the stereo imaging wasn't dramatic enough. Alaskan habitats are difficult because the creature voice density along the coast is light. It sometimes takes time to capture just the right textures in that type of environment. After many tries, I captured enough sounds to produce the first third of the album early one morning, in one session, and from one spot. The final two-thirds of the CD are composite mixes made up of various recorded elements.

I took my time, never rushing, never feeling pressured in the field. Recording is a meditative process. I had the first twenty minutes on tape but only separate parts for the rest and had to build them track-by-track into a cohesive piece in the studio. I considered many forms of expression, ranging from an album that might include tracks representing individual species, movement through time (day-night, seasons), movement through space (from site-to-site). In the end, considering the wide range of material I had collected, I chose to create a spatial representation. That's because the greater Glacier Bay ecosystem extends fifty-five miles from north to south and includes extensive territory beyond the bay, itself. A grizzly bear was recorded on Willoughby Island, and killer whales were recorded attacking a humpback in Finger's Bay. Additional wolves were recorded one morning near the western border of Glacier Bay National Preserve.

Calving glaciers were recorded further north off the Hubbard Glacier east of Yakutat.

I assembled these parts imagining what someone might experience in a day in the Alaskan wilderness. The first twenty minutes, a single recording, begins with thrushes, eagles and wolves in the background. The spatial journey takes the listener past the water's edge and the "blows" of humpback whales at our campsite, a few yards from where I had set up my mic. At that point, the illusion becomes a composite that travels aurally over land to glacial habitats where we hear calving of the glaciers creating their own special geophony. From a distance, they sound like deadened explosions, when a wall of ice, towering five hundred feet, breaks from the leading edge and crashes to the water at its base. At one point, I lowered myself down into the crevasse (described earlier) a couple of miles inland from the face where we had hiked. With my hydrophone buried in some dirt-laden ice melt at my feet, I managed to record the very low frequency sound of the glacial mass as it moved over the terrain, perhaps the first ever of that type of recording. This, too, is featured in the soundscape, as are all the other elements. The idea was to seamlessly represent the more dynamic acoustic properties of the region, while, at the same time, not stranding the listener with repetitive sounds that could, over time, become boring or distracting.

At the eastern foot of the Askinuk Mountains my wife and I recorded the Alaskan tundra late one spring. Just past the peak of the nesting season, there was still plenty of bird action. Everywhere we walked, birds were nesting in the vegetation, completely unperturbed by our presence. Among them were the savanna sparrow, dark-eyed junco, Wilson's warbler, yellow wagtail, ruby-crowned kinglet, wheatear, snipe, long-tailed jaeger, and mergansers. We also sighted and recorded a nesting pair of Arctic loons. Instead of many segments and a complicated mix, this album was done with virtually no studio editing (meaning cutting) and by segueing together a few cohesive long recorded samples (about four). Yet, I do not consider myself a purist for doing this. It was just —like all others—an editing choice.

Production Philosophies

There are currently two basic mixing—or element combining—philosophies; the first posits that without any editing (meaning cutting tape or changing sequences of time), a recordist/producer is able to present a more "pure" unadulterated example of a particular natural soundscape. The other philosophy holds that all recordings have been edited in some manner. The "purist" claims are both misleading and disingenuous. As mentioned earlier, the very act of selecting sounds to record, restricts or "edits" the result you will ultimately hear. From the minute you push the "record" button, you have transformed the sound. What is important is that the result is credible and engaging. In the final analysis, whether or not actual post-production editing or mixing takes place, a compelling and engaging result is both the goal and primary measure of a recorded soundscape's worth.

Making Creative Decisions

With the raw field recordings in hand, you need to determine how you want to use your material. This may determine how you store it, whether on a CD, DAT, DVD, or other medium. Audio mixes—combinations of long and short audio samples—can be stored on a hard drive, DAT, CD, CD-ROM, DVD, and on video and film soundtracks. Once you determine whether the mix will be designed for CDs, public spaces (interpretative exhibits), multi-media presentations, web sites, or interactive displays, you have a number of options to consider. Sound is currently and generally relegated to any of several media: CDs, DVDs, program material stored on hard (or zip) drives for playback, and into MP3 or Flash formats for web applications. Sometimes your audio program is designed to be stored on DAT cassettes, and almost never these days on standard audio cassette. Tape-based media have proven to be far more problematic and less stable for storage and frequent playback.

In the production phase, where you wish to re-create the soundscape of a particular habitat, the obvious main choices aside from the more common species-specific, are time and space. You can do one or the other; even both in the same mix.

How to use time

With natural soundscapes, time is represented by creating a mix that features, for example, a dawn-to-dusk or spring-to-fall representation. It can also feature a short period of elapsed time like a dawn-to-daytime chorus or an evening-to-dark chorus. (In real time, some dawn choruses take as little as 20 minutes while others can take well over an hour.) A natural soundscape can be seasonal, winter through spring, or summer and fall in a given habitat, or it can represent an annual cycle.

How to use space

You can take the listener on a journey from the seashore on the beach, under the surface of the ocean, down into the pelagic depths, then back to the beach, once again. Or you can follow a drop of water from its source in the mountains, along its entire course through several biomes all its way to the sea.

How to combine time and space

Take your listener on a journey through both time and space; for example, the journey might begin with springtime in the valley floor of the Grand Teton mountain range, and travel into the summer and the nearby bio-regions of Yellowstone National Park.

Exploring varied biomes within habitats

Some extreme locations, like the Arctic, Antarctic, or some desert regions, cannot easily be represented by any of the above examples. In that case, it is best to break up the zones into distinct cuts each representing a particular acoustic element of a varied habitat. Sometimes this is best expressed as species-specific recordings. Doug Quin does this on his album, *Antarctica*.[2] He felt that it was too much of an aesthetic stretch to try to combine Weddell seals and Emperor penguins within the same soundscape because they were so singular and unique. They worked better on his CD when separated.

> *The pheasant cries out from the door of its nest...*
> *Crying out from the door, at the sound of the coming rain...*
> *Rain and wind from the west, spreading over the country...*
> *It cries out, perched on the top rails of the huts.*
> *It is always there, at the wide expanse of water, listening for the rising*
>   *wind and rain:*
> *Wind and rain from the west, as the pheasant cries out...*
>
> —Arnhem Land, Australia

1. Mathieu, W. A. *The Musical Life: Reflections on What Is and How to Live It.* (Shambala Press: Boston & London, 1994.)

2. Quin, Doug. *Antarctica* (compact disc recording). (Wild Sanctuary: Glen Ellen, CA, 1998.)

CHAPTER 12

Bioregions and Sounds to Explore

At Play in the Fields

The world leaves no track in space,

and the greatest action of man leaves no mark in the vast idea.

—Ralph Waldo Emerson

 Marine and terrestrial environments explode with sound. Within these two main earth environments, there are many, many transitional zones called *ecotones* that feature wonderful biomes. An ecotone literally means a transitional zone between one type of biome, or area typified by certain life forms, and another. It can be a large area or a micro-habitat. In the ecotone, you will find plants and animals that are characteristic of their bordering biomes.

The exploration of sound reveals how many different types of rainforest, desert, and temperate zones can be distinguished. For example, marine environments include—fresh water lakes, ponds, puddles, pelagic (open seas), and littoral ocean habitats, and still-living coral reefs: all alive with a variety of sounds. There are also transitional marine environments such as inter-tidal areas, tidepools, and places like mangrove swamps, coastal chaparral, secondary and tertiary dune zones, and island habitats. *Riparian*, or fresh water habitats, range from small creeks that have very little water in them to roaring high mountain streams or the wide muddy rivers of the mid-west. On terra firma, there are a number of remarkably diverse environments from arid deserts to lush tropics and sub-tropical areas, from broad prairies to dense woodlands, from the arctic and sub-arctic areas to more temperate zones.

It is hard to name one's favorite place among such diversity, but most of us have at least one or two locations that excite or welcome us more than any other. Alaska is that exemplary place for me: it contains *everything*— from rainforests to some of the most exciting marine life on the planet. Since it is still sparsely populated, it tends to be a relatively quiet place to record. Part of the discovery of wild soundscapes is finding what places are special to *you*. Through the adventure of sound recording, you come to know these places more intimately.

> *I will arise and go now, and go to Innisfree,*
> *And a small cabin build there, of clay and wattles made:*
> *Nine bean-rows will I have there, a hive for the honey-bee,*
> *And live alone in the bee-loud glade.*
>
> *And I shall have some peace there, for peace comes dropping slow,*
> *Dropping from the veils of the morning to where the crickets sings;*
> *There midnight's all a glimmer, and noon a purple glow,*
> *And evening full of the linnet's wings.*
>
> *I will arise and go now, for always night and day*
> *I hear lake water lapping with low sounds by the shore;*
> *While I stand on the roadway, or on the pavements grey,*
> *I hear it in the deep heart's core.*

William Butler Yeats, "The Lake Isle of Innisfree"

In this chapter, we'll explore some specific bioregions and locations and examine the opportunities they present for capturing wild sounds. I'll range far afield, often to exotic places few may ever have a chance to see. Many of the places mentioned are featured on the CD that accompanies this book. I invite you to imagine how these exquisite environments express themselves, how each is intricate and complex, how each is unique.

Some Specific Biomes to Explore

Deserts (American)

In the Americas, desert regions stretch from central Mexico up through much of Utah, Colorado, Nevada and central California. A great deal of creature sound obviously depends on each area's altitude, climate and available food and water supplies. Nevertheless, there are many vocal insects, birds, mammals, and even reptiles to be found in what many mistakenly believe is a desolate place.

The average tourist drives across the desert to get to the other side and misses much of the action. If you fly by at 70 miles per hour looking out the window of your car or recreational vehicle, you may only see flashes of occasional scrub and cactus set upon mounds of sand or crusted soil. Industry and government often see the desert as uninhabited land waiting to be exploited or developed, or as a dumping ground for nuclear and other waste disposal. The mining industry digs the precious ores that are buried in desert mountains and caves. The military shells and bombs it, and uses it as a test site or landing strip. And then, there are those who delight in shattering the desert's dead silence with roaring dune buggies, dirt bikes, and overland recreational vehicles. But, the desert is a fragile landscape, and in need of protection. In many parks, hikers are instructed to stay strictly on paths that wind through forests of cacti and porous rock because of the diatomaceous earth that is alive with microscopic cells. A footstep on the desert can leave a lasting trace.

Deserts are alive with the voices of many kinds of creatures and environmental sounds, if you learn how to listen for them out beyond the seeming silence of the desert air. Here are a few examples of deserts where I have recorded natural sounds. Most of them are in the southwestern United States, but you can explore other desert biomes further north and east toward the Rocky Mountains. The Great Basin Desert reaches Idaho, southeastern Oregon, western Utah and northern Nevada. Much of northern and north-central Mexico is also a desert region.

The Sonoran-Chihuahuan high desert is located in the panhandle of New Mexico *(CD Track 11)*. It is the only location in the Lower Forty-Eight states where it can be completely noise-free for extended periods of time. Within an area of five square miles, this bioregion contains many different mini-biomes, each characterized by distinctive biophonic zones. In the throes of recovery from several hundred years of over-grazing, this is a place where older bioacoustic paradigms might not apply. Each mini-biome contains its own mix of vocal creatures, and includes certain plants that attract creatures who are specially adapted to survive in the harsh desert conditions and climate. Some of the plants you will find in the Sonoran-Chihuahuan high desert include aspens, juniper and oak, mesquite, cactus, manzanita, alder, hackberry, shrub, Indian rice- and sawgrasses, broom, sage, arrow weed, and ocotillo.

You may discover and record a number of species of birds in this area, including: cactus and rock wrens; common and Chihuahuan ravens; western meadowlarks; house finches; Brewer's, sage, and chipping sparrows; green-tailed towhees; blue grosbeaks; longspurs; loggerhead shrike; vermilion and ash-throated flycatchers; horned larks; western kingbirds; common poorwills. There are also burrowing and great horned owls; ground doves; aplomado falcons and red-tailed hawks; and scaled quails.

Other creatures who call the Sonoran-Chihuahuan desert their home are coyotes, gray foxes, mountain lions, jack rabbits, squirrels, bats, mice, ants, toads and frogs of many types, geckos, tortoises, and snakes. Insects include katydids, beetles, ants, termites, grasshoppers, crickets and Mormon crickets. Each creature has a singularly expressive voice and the zones in which they live are alive with enchanting creature choruses.

Having heard how desolate and dead most deserts were, I was rewarded with many spectacular epiphanies here. Listening—perhaps more than any other sense—demonstrates that, in spite of our search for life in outer space, there's a planet right here, teeming with life forms that we still know practically nothing about. The desert is a wonderful place to learn to listen if you can get far enough away from roads, the water pumps of farms and ranches, the mechanical "grasshoppers" pumping for oil, the roar of recreational vehicles, and the sounds of domesticated animals.

The Mojave Desert in southeastern California is another great desert to explore and has many good recording sites. Start your sound safari at campsites located at Granite Pass, on Kelbaker Road off of Hwy. 40, between Barstow and Needles, California. The campsites are situated to the west as you come to the top of the pass from the south. From them, you can find accessible trails into the Granite Mountains. There are lots of birds, wild burros, and ringtails, to see, listen to, and record.

Five and a half miles north on Kelbaker Road, is the cutoff for the Kelso Dunes, famous for their singing (see Chapter 9). If you decide to record dunes, bear in mind that the dune surfaces tend to be windy; mics will not generally tolerate bluster unless their patterns are omnidirectional. Nor do mics tolerate sand. Another way to help lessen the effect of wind in your microphone is to introduce a *filter* into the line between your mic and the sound source before the signal reaches the recorder. By filtering out the low frequency below 100Hz, the wind's effect is greatly relieved. Some mics have a low-frequency filter switch as an integral part of the system that can be activated. Some upper-end DAT recorders supply a filter at the mic input. And some systems require an outboard microphone pre-amplifier with a filter included.

From the Mojave Desert, it's about 120 miles north to Death Valley Junction, an area I would not recommend because it is too well-traveled and there are no booming dunes (that I know of). If you can find a way up into the Amargosa Range, which borders Nevada on the east and the Panamints in the west, you will find that it is protected from traffic noise and maybe you will hear coyotes and discover enough wildlife to record.

Mono Lake is another great desert site set in the rain-shadow of the eastern Sierra Nevada mountains in California. It is typical of a high desert bioregion. Mono is located off Highway 395, the main north-south highway along California's eastern edge, or via Tioga Pass, east of Yosemite. An eerily placid lake, Mono is famous for its magical tufa towers and wonderful but sometimes windy habitat, which makes recording a bit of a challenge. I've recorded spade foot toads not far from the hot springs at the north side of the lake since 1984. Until the mid-1990s, one could record there with no problem. By then, the number of toads had considerably diminished; it was obvious that something was amiss. The Forest Service, along with volunteers from the Mono Lake Committee, rebuilt parts of the fragile habitat by replanting native grasses and allowing more water flow so that the toads and other wildlife could co-exist throughout their respective cycles thus replenishing their threatened populations. Professional recordists need to get a permit to record there now although no permit is needed if your purpose is non-commercial. However, the Bureau of Land Management (BLM) and National Park Service (NPS) distinguish between commercial and non-commercial by the number of legs you mount under your mic or camera. If you use a tripod, your purpose is automatically deemed commercial. In addition, there are strict rules about how close you can camp to the water's edge. Nevertheless, this area is worth capturing on tape as long as you tread lightly and stay aware of the rules by talking with the local Forest Service rangers. Your recordings of spade foot toads, a very unusual creature with great performance skills, and red-winged black birds, water fowl, and California gulls, will be something to hear!

Nevada's Ruby Mountains are located along Highway 80, south of Wells, Nevada, about three hours west of Salt Lake City and ten hours east of San Francisco. This is another great high mountain desert location but you need to arrive early in the spring to avoid other campers, hikers, and recreational vehicles. There are two accessible sites where you can begin your sound explorations. One is on the western side a mile to the southwest of Lamoille. Take a road marked FR 660 (Lamoille Canyon Rd.) toward Ruby Crest National Recreation Area to find campsites. However, unless you want to focus on recording streams, you will need to find better and quieter places to listen, observe, and record. If the snow has melted, there may be campers and pick-up trucks heading toward the top here; consequently, they add noise to the environment that may interfere with your efforts to hear and record the *wild* soundscape.

The ridge-line trail lets you hike to spectacular views, good recording sites (when the wind is light), and solitude. On the eastern side of the mountain, you will find more campsites and a fine place to record. To reach this area, also accessible south of Wells, take Highway 93 south to 229 west; here, 229 dead ends, so turn south on the dirt road. Take any of the accessible Forest Service roads (you'll definitely need four-wheel drive, a good pair of legs, or both, and go west up the hill to find a campsite). For those who like to hike and wish to find great spring and early summer locations to record, there are many trails, and terrific bird, mammal, and insect sites to be heard at this spot in the Ruby Mountain area.

Deserts (Outside of the U.S.)

Deserts exist in many parts of the world, and because of climatic changes, they are expanding rapidly. I haven't been to many off-shore except for the high desert of the Masai Mara in Kenya, and Australia, where the Pitjanjara (aborigines) tell of finding directions from place to place by listening to the green ants sing. When I tried this, I got lost not two miles into my biophonic walkabout. I didn't have a clue how to listen in the subtle ways of the Pitjanjara. When I came limping back, they laughed (hard) as I nursed a bad case of crushed ego and a sunburn for more days than I want to count. If you have the money and the inclination to travel, try the Skeleton Coast in Namibia, some desert island habitats, parts of the Sahara and the Sinai, and the coastal desert of Peru.

Rainforests

North Americans commonly think of rainforests as being steamy, hot, and tropical, and located primarily along the equator. Few realize that rainforest biophonies express themselves as far south as the edge of Rio de Janeiro (*technically*, though many have now been damaged or destroyed), and stretch along the coasts of Northern California, Oregon, Washington and British Columbia coasts, as far north as Anchorage, Alaska. A rainforest may be "dry," about ninety inches of rain each year, or wet with hundreds of inches of rain instead, but even the dry ones are pretty wet.

Elsewhere in the United States, rainforests and swamps exist in the southeast, from the Cypress Creek in Georgia, the Everglades and Corkscrew Swamp of Florida, to the bayous of Louisiana. These are fairly easy for many people to travel to and they are fun places to explore and record. Because of the denser populations in those parts of the country, however, they are also fairly noisy with aircraft, watercraft, and automobile traffic. If you begin early in the day or late at night, you will find quiet intervals that will prove rewarding in your quest for natural sound. Other rainforest environments are found in areas of the world that are more difficult to get to, though no less rewarding. Some of these are described below.

Australia has a terrific riverine rainforest habitat, upriver from Port Douglas in the northeast corner of Australia, replete with birds, crocodiles, ants, reptiles, amphibians, and crustaceans (including snapping shrimp) *(CD Track 12)*. At locations like these you will find both enchanting and disturbing moments such as I did one afternoon when I witnessed a crocodile purloining a poodle when the dog went down to the river to get a drink. As with many other habitats in Australia, this one is under siege, diminishing with each passing year, and in danger of being altered and depleted within a short period of time. It is difficult to get far enough away from motorized river vessels no matter how far you walk into the forest. Nor is there a time (even at two in the morning) that the human-induced noises cease for more than a few minutes.

The Amazon, in South America, is a challenging and potentially dangerous place to explore and record, but it is rich in wild soundscapes. As you walk through any rainforest or jungle territory, at any time of day or night (especially where there might be poisonous snakes), you learn to shine a light into dark coverts, under logs and foliage, to walk at a careful pace, and to pay *extremely* close attention. You also learn how to protect yourself and your gear from the unexpected. No matter how well trained or how proficient you think you are, being alone in such a place is guaranteed to raise your pulse rate by several hundred percent. In tropical rainforests you must be sensitive to information that any one your senses offer: sight, smell, the tactile, and aural. Add to those your kinesthetic, intuitive, and any other sense you think you may have, and use them all.

The scent of a jaguar is especially characteristic here and a smell you want to notice. Most members of the feline family spray to mark their territory. In the case of *Panthera onca*, the scent it leaves is noticeable, even from a distance. Trying to record jaguars in their home territory is not recommend. This large cat is, pound for pound, one of the strongest creatures in the mammal kingdom. It can drag a horse several times its weight many miles through the forest. One night while recording there, I picked up a jaguar's scent as it followed me down a trail—the animal was well out of sight. No sooner had I set up my mic than the cat stepped up to it and began to sniff, chuff, and growl *(CD Track 10)*. With some luck, I have lived to tell about it. Anytime you want to record a jaguar,

I know a certain trail...

The Rio Doce or the Caratinga region, in South America just north of Rio de Janeiro, is a dry tropical rainforest known for its unusual monkeys, including the large howlers (*Alouatta fusca*), and the beautiful, tiny, golden lion tamarins (*Leontopithecus rosalia*), as well as for many unique birds and insects. This dry rainforest is a remnant of a larger one that once covered about 1,500 miles between southern Amazonia and Rio de Janeiro. Now reduced to about eighteen square miles, this biological "island" is now an important research site, yet its boundaries are constantly besieged by farmers and those who live just outside the borders who harvest the once-abundant hardwood fuel and poach wild plants and animals with impunity.

The biophonies heard here include the vocalizations of the parauque, great kiskadee, rufus bellied thrush, white crested guan, common potoo, yellow-throated spinetail, tropical screech owl, spectacled owl, pygmy owl, black-bellied tree duck, slaty ant shrike, Amazonian antpitta, and the sounds of terrific parrot flyovers. A wide variety of frogs and several different species of ants also vocalize in this rainforest. As with many research sites, the biologists here built one hundred-meter grids within the forest that have been marked by paths between locations. The acoustic boundaries, however, are shaped quite differently; they do not follow the rational human structures we try to impose on the natural world. Instead, these biophonic territories are more amoeba-shaped—sometimes as small as 100 square meters (approximately 110 square yards). The boundaries expand, contract, and change shape according to times of day and night, seasons, and weather. It is possible to discover bioacoustic zones as large as half a mile or more.

◉)) Try This: Map It Yourself!

Traditional research models often do not fit the boundaries of a true biome. Sometimes you must disregard them and map the biome yourself, paying close attention to the relative biophonies. This is really fun to do, whether or not you are recording.

As you walk through a given habitat, note the changes in the biophony—especially the transitional zones, the *ecotones*, where one territory blends into another. There are regional consistencies you will begin to recognize—things that remain constant—and other sounds that will change as you move through the territory. This appears to be true for most environments—not only rainforests.

Indonesia, an island nation in the southeast Pacific Ocean below the China Sea, contains a wide variety of rainforest habitats from wet to dry. The enhanced sonic world that you can discover in places like Sumatra or Borneo will take you deep into the rainforest both physically and emotionally. Gibbons, siamangs, orangutans, leaf monkeys, mustached babbler, white-rumped shama, rhinoceros hornbills, Argus pheasants, insects and frogs all appear to be much more present when amplified through microphones than what you are able to hear unassisted.

In Sumatra, you might spot a rare clouded leopard as it stalks through dense vegetation. Of all the leopard's finely distinguished rosette patterns and cat-like features, its beautiful shape and grace as it glides eloquently by, nothing stands out more than watching its smallish, flat ears catch every nuance of moment and sound. Every twig, each slight puff of air, even the sound of your eyes blinking will catch its attention. In Borneo (*CD Track 13*), you can hire a river boat to Camp Leakey. While you may not find creature comforts on such a trip, the experience is gratifying (except for the noisy boat engine). When the captain pulls to shore, you can stretch your legs, then walk a mile or so away from the river to set up your mics in the forest and record.

))) Borneo—An Imaginary Sound Safari

It is quiet in the jungle most afternoons. Very still.
No birds. Not even mosquitoes. Only a few lightly
voiced cicadas, so soft that they create a sense that
something is about to happen. It gets quieter. At first,
you don't notice the cumulus clouds looming in the
distance and heading toward you because of the forest canopy. But the creatures certainly do. The electric-
ity in the air is palpable. By their silence, the creatures
are telling you something. Oblivious, you record the
eerie stillness. Except for your breathing, it's dead
quiet with not even the slightest movement register-
ing on the recorder's level meter, so you crank up the
mic input volume to catch whatever sound is there.

The first colossal hit of lightning and thunder is so
close and so loud that it shatters a nearby tree and
nearly blows out the input to your recorder. Any closer
and you would have been fried because you forgot to
take your headphones off—a no-no during a storm.
Thinking you'll catch the next clap of thunder you turn
the input levels WAY down and detach the phones
from your recorder. As soon as you do, the next thunder crack hits, this time further away, but loud nevertheless. Luck is with you this time—you catch the
event on tape. A few seconds later, you get another
great ear-shattering boom.

The storm builds to a grand crescendo. The
approaching rain creating a whoosh that seems distant at first, then it careens toward you. It creates a
Doppler effect that rises in pitch and cuts through the
forest with the impact of a speeding freight train.
When the highest intensity reaches your shelter, it virtually pins the level meters on the recorder and you
have to back off your already low-set levels to avoid
overloading the input. A terrific moment.

Just as it had moved swiftly toward you, the storm
recedes—all of this drama occurring over a few short
minutes. The rain has grown gentle and fairly drips
onto the forest vegetation. The thunder rolls grow

even more distant, the insect sounds reappear amidst the rhythm of post-storm drips. Then, the first late afternoon birds begin to sing, followed by others who join in the chorus. In the relentless humidity and heat there is a feeling of release and freshness expressed by the biophony and the sweet scent of the forest. Reinvigorated and relaxed at the same time, you amble back to your boat and head toward another site or your base camp.

Costa Rica has the San Juan River floodplain on its Osa Peninsula where there is a *mangrove* swamp with about a six-foot tidal change. In the evening, you can set up your mics alongside the road at the time of the receding tide. You will hear popping and dripping sounds coming from the tendrils of the mangrove vegetation. You'll also hear bats, mosquitoes, the glorious mix of insects, tinamous, various types of tree frog action, and some owls. As with other rainforest conditions, you will want to make certain that you have the type of microphone that will not be subject to imminent failure from an overdose of humidity. If you shine a light on the popping and dripping sounds, you may discover the source. The clamor comes from families of crabs letting go of the vines and falling several feet into the outgoing tide water and mud below because their bodies need to stay moist *(CD Track 14)*.

The rainforests of high equatorial Africa, in places like Rwanda or Uganda and the Virunga Mountains, are incredible for recording the remaining groups of mountain gorillas. These areas are not easy to get to, and not necessarily safe, but they are worth the risk and the money. You need to be in good health and physical condition, and it helps to have an adventurous soul. The trackers, researchers, and visitors sometimes trudge three or four miles up and down steep mountainous terrain, between eight and twelve thousand feet, knee deep in secondary growth vines and stinging nettles, mud, and other vegetation to finally catch up with the gorillas. You have to learn the type of high-step necessary for walking through this unique mountain rainforest.

Each gorilla group eats through a quarter mile of vegetation every day. They find a nest where they bed down around midday, then they eat some more before settling into another nesting site for the evening. By morning they are usually several miles from the previous day's site. Because the gorillas tend to travel great distances, any equipment you take needs to be as light as possible and made up of components that are easy to set up and tear down. When a gorilla curiously approaches a microphone or other piece of equipment out of curiosity, you will want to have it placed outside their reach. As they move, you will regularly have to re-position yourself so that you are able to catch whatever infrequent vocalizations are uttered. That means tearing down and setting up your equipment many times each hour.

I was recording with my back to Pablo, a large silverback gorilla, when I heard a crash of vegetation. Because my mikes are stereo, I could only get a sense of the sound coming from either right or left; I had no way of knowing that the sound came from directly behind me. I discovered that when Pablo's forceful hand grabbed my right shoulder, picked me up—equipment and all—and flung me fifteen feet into a patch of stinging nettles! ...Other than the stinging nettles that brushed my face when I landed, I experienced no pain from the fall, only a profound sense of awe. Pablo was only clearing a path as he moved to attack another gorilla and I happened to be one of several objects in the way.

—Journal entry, Rwanda, Africa

With currently available technology, you could easily travel and record for a month or more in the field with about ten additional pounds added to your normal field gear. A DAT or mini-disc recorder fits in a pocket. The mic cable can be reduced to a single coaxial stereo line, and the headphones are unencumbered. Best of all, one charge of a good gel cell battery lasts about fifteen hours and weighs two-and-one-quarter pounds. Depending on use, two battery packs are all that would normally be needed. DAT tape—all sixteen hours worth—weighs a total of one pound, but each one lasts ninety minutes (the recommended format). Because either a DAT or mini-disc system is easy to set up and tear down (about thirty seconds each way), capturing the sounds poses no problem if the animals happen to be vocalizing. In most cases, as with gorillas on the move, I would probably just stuff the whole shebang into a large pocket or day-pack still plugged in, and move to the next site right along with them.

Oceans

When you stand on the seashore looking out at the waves, you might think it would be easy to record the sound of the ocean. This type of biome, after all, seems straightforward to hear, and if you live within a reasonable distance its sound is all pervasive, all encompassing. Yet, one of my biggest surprises in the field of recording was my inability to capture on tape what I was experiencing with my ears. Every time I went to the shore to record, I placed a mic where (after listening and planning for what I felt was an appropriate amount of time) I was hearing the best expression of ocean waves. Each time I returned to my studio and played back the recordings, they failed to evoke what I had heard and what I was expecting. In fact, the sound was so thin, so lacking in presence or dynamic, at first I thought it was my mic system.

I was younger then, and believed fully in the divinity of technology coupled with the efficacy of our large brain. So I invested in more and more elaborate and expensive mics (all recommended by professional colleagues), went more often to the shore to record and capture the elusive ocean signature and came home only to be disappointed again and again. It turns out that the problem was not with the microphones, at all. It was with the way I had been taught to listen. As I described earlier in this book, I was conditioned to hear what I was *looking* at. When I looked directly at waves breaking in the distance, I heard the deep thunderous low-frequency roar as the waves curled and pounded into the surf. When I looked at the near-field where the waves were breaking closer to shore, I heard more detail—and there was a larger sense of water movement. And when, at last, I would see the lip of the waves moving up the rake of the beach with the leading edge stopping at my feet, I distinctly heard the tiny bubbles bursting as the water moved over the surface of the sand. It was only when I closed my eyes that my mind translated the sound into something approaching the compelling and resonant voice I had come to the beach to hear, after all.

It took me ten years of trial and error to realize what I had been neglecting with my mics and recorders. The truth is that, no matter how expensive and no matter what the claims, all of these tools are quite limited. Each component has been designed for a special limited purpose based on certain criteria that designers incorporate into their respective products. No microphone picks up everything. If you want to reduce the sound of the ocean to a CD recording, or even approach the illusion of how it sounds when waves hit the shore, you will need to record the surf from many different perspectives—near-field detail, mid-field detail, and distant components. Once these are on tape, they need to be recombined in the studio in order to create the chimera of the ocean's voice that will convince a skeptical listener that you were there.

Former president Ronald Reagan once flippantly remarked that, "If you've seen one redwood, you've seen 'em all." I am often asked if all oceans *sound* alike. To the untrained ear, perhaps, insect, frog, or bird choruses may sound very similar at first. However, one of the fascinating things about recording, revealed by my experience of trying record the ocean, is that waves at the shore may sound quite different from place to place. First, there's the occasional ambient sound of shore birds that triggers a sense of locale. Different beaches, different secondary and tertiary dune grasses, different on-shore habitat and climate, different creature mixes provide specific and unique clues. Secondly, the rake of the beach, its slant as it moves up from the water, affects wave action and creates contrasts that register on tape. Some beaches have very active, even violent action; others sound more gentle. Finally, the rhythm of the waves differs from beach to beach, high tide to low, stormy to calm, and from season to season. Each site has its own distinctive range of signatures and performances. It is even possible that creatures may be partially drawn to the special geophony of particular coastal sites. In other words, the geographical features of a location may contribute to, inspire, or inhibit, the creatures' performance of sound.

Fresh Water Habitats

As ocean coastal shorelines sound different, so do inland fresh water lakes for much the same reasons. With fresh water habitats, the wave movement tends to be more gentle on average, with more of a quick rhythmic lapping staccato sound.

Beaches

I've recorded beaches at the tip of Latin America, in Africa, Madagascar, the Azorés, New Zealand, Australia, Fiji, and the west coast of North America from Baja California to Alaska, including beaches by large fresh water lakes. When I rack them up to audition, and listen to them side-to-side, they all sound different. While weather and other conditions vary, recordings may be done in the same manner as you invest in and create your blend of tools and equipment. When my beach samples were recorded, they weren't done with the idea of being used for comparisons. Since

none of the samples match, it's my guess
that, contrary to what the former president said about trees, if you've heard
one beach, you've (only) heard the
unique geophony of one beach.

Islands

You will discover a wide variety of
creature sound experiences on the
various islands of the world that
combine desert and tropical rainforest biomes. Vanua Levu, one of
the large islands within the Fijian
chain, is a rare and quiet location to
record. This is a dry riparian habitat
on a hill that faces north about two
kilometers from the ocean. It has
been partially clear-cut and this, of
course, has affected the aural atmos-
phere. The dawn chorus here is lovely
but scant, due perhaps to sparse vegetation and the severe erosion caused by
human habitation in evidence everywhere.
In the early dawn light you may hear the Fiji
wood swallow, gray-backed white-eye, and sever-
al other species of birds. The silhouette of a huge bat gliding
on the gentle currents offshore with an incredible wingspread the size of a
turkey vulture is a common sight. Just offshore, magnificent coral reef systems play host to many kinds of sea creatures just below the surface of the
water. In the crystal clear water, creatures are visible from above so they can
be identified.

Wave action is often light enough here so that you can drop a
hydrophone over the side of your boat to hear the sounds of damselfish, the
three spot daesyllus, parrot fish, wrasses, puffers, cardinals, fusiliers, goat-
fish, crustaceans, and butterfly fish—all part of the reef biophony. The
cracking, spitting, grunting, and percussive sounds all mix together in a
staccato rhythm that will bring a smile to your face.

Mountains

Mountain habitats, in general, pose special problems for sound
recordists. Where there is wildlife, there are usually streams, which create
distracting noise if you are trying to emphasize creature biophonies. There
may be strong wind, with its sound moving through the forest canopy and
other vegetation. Where there are roads, there's usually a considerable
amount of deforestation and the consequent reductions in creature presence. Where there are backcountry trails, there may be light or commercial

aircraft (noise, again). Other noisy disruptions in the mountains, especially near campsites, cabin villages, or small towns, include dirt bikes, chain saws, boom boxes, radios, domestic animals, automobiles and snowmobiles. If you are near a lake that allows motor boats, you will have those sounds to contend with as well. These obstacles are particularly evident in North American mountains. Nevertheless, like most people, I love the mountains too much to give up the chance of discovering great places to listen there.

Yellowstone National Park, with its mountains, lakes, rivers, and valleys, is one of the most exciting places to record, particularly in the fall when you may be able to hear and record wolves and elk *(CD Track 16)*. Find a good location at the northeastern end of the Lamar Valley, where the Druid pack of wolves are occasionally spotted. This area tends to be less crowded, especially in the off-season; therefore, it generates less noise than other areas of the park. From the Pebble Creek campsite, hike away from the stream to the northwest, away from the main trail. You will arrive at a series of open meadows. Hide yourself in the treeline, upwind from where you hear elks' bugling. Hope that the elk won't catch your scent—it's a bit like hoping the sun won't rise in the east—then, set up your recording system and wait.

Elk have learned about predators over time. Never mind that you are armed only with recorders. The re-introduction of wolves into Yellowstone has heightened the elks' levels of alertness, so they are easily spooked. Remain very still and quiet. Since they often pass through that area, you may be lucky enough to hear the bugling up close. It takes patience —you might need several days to capture just the right sound. Dawn is the best time to try this, although elk bugle at dusk and at other times of the day. The best time to make this visit is between mid-September and early October, but be prepared for snow in Yellowstone anytime after August.

Along the edge habitats of the meadows, you can also record the fall voices of ravens, grouse, a merlin, cedar waxwings, geese, Downy woodpeckers, juncos, larks, house sparrows, and king-birds. Yellowstone is a thousand miles from where I live, but I'd make the trip once a week if I had the money for gas.

Grand Teton National Park in Wyoming is another mountain zone worth exploring. Adjacent to Yellowstone, it's another great place to listen for the bugling of elk. As you reach the park entrance at Moose, Wyoming, north of Jackson, follow your park service map to White Grass Meadows and hear the bugling at dusk. The Tetons comprise the only national park with a full-service jet-sanctioned airport located right in the middle of the valley. There is a *lot* of noise. When a 737 or private jet takes off, it can be heard ten miles away. (This, incidentally, is the new fly-in home of many movie stars — some of them claiming to be environmentalists — who moved to Jackson to avoid the noise and urbanization of Aspen, Vail, and Los Angeles.) White Grass Meadows also comes with some stream noise. So, while this is may not be the best place to record, it is a great place to listen and observe the elk.

Never give up your search for quiet places to record. On a dirt road leading to the east, about 18 miles north of Moose junction off of Highway 191, you should find "FR 30310" (on your friendly DeLorme map of Wyoming). Follow this forest road around to the north (stay to the left where the roads fork) and then east for about five miles. You'll come to a watershed where there are marshes, a small pond and some edge habitat that has more creatures than you can think of: frogs, birds, insects, and mammals. Plus, it's in the *noise-shadow* of most of the Jackson Hole valley. You can record both fresh water marine and terrestrial habitats and discover some terrific wildlife soundscapes including elk. In addition, a newly released pack of wolves is reported to be in the vicinity. You just might hear them and be the first to record their howls.

Grasslands and Plains

Wind is a constant challenge when trying to record creatures and sounds. Yet, wind is characteristic of the soundscapes that you will often hear in grasslands, prairies or plains. Primary sound effects result from wind through the trees, wind in the grasses, and pitched wind (wind that changes tone). For wind in the trees, find some aspens (called "quakies" in the American West). They really *do* quake — gently. When you get right under a young aspen, one with shimmering leaf-filled branches not more than eight feet above the ground, you might get a recording that will *sound* like leaves blowing in the wind. You may end up with a recording that sounds more like close-up surf, or rain, or something not-quite-wind-like and indistinct, because wind through trees is a difficult thing to record. My best aspen recordings were made on Trail Creek Road (FR208), heading east from Ketchum, Idaho. At the top of the ridge in the Challis National Forest, there are a number of sites just off the road where you can record for short periods (intermittent traffic interrupts the wild soundscape). You might do as I did once and park your car under the tree where you want to record. The car's body works as a shelter for the mics, protecting them from the gusts blowing at the top of the ridge. The subsequent recording sounds just like what you would imagine wind in the trees to sound like. Note, that by changing levels from low to high, you can give the impression of light breezes to high, gale-force blows, and everything in between.

With most recordings, it's really quite difficult to distinguish wind in the trees from wind in grasses. But there is a distinction. When grasses are recorded properly, they tend to sound much closer to the components of rain than well-recorded shafts of vegetation. That's because when the leaves of grass hit each other in the wind, the result is more one of friction and release than percussion. Contact between blades tends to be very light and the resultant sound is high pitched. If you can get your mics in position to capture the illusion, you've succeeded.

Experiment with different mics to identify those that create your desired impression. Remember to keep your mics out of the direct force of the wind, by getting them close to, or directly on, the ground. Lavaliere mics are probably best for this purpose. If you're using omni-directional lavaliere mics, you might try attaching them to a particularly strong leaf of grass or the small branch of a nearby low-lying bush. I think ground level is better; that way, if all conditions conspire in your favor, you will get a good recording. Monitor the sound through your headphones with your eyes closed. If you have your mics positioned correctly and they are picking up wind effect blowing through the grass along with the light "clicks" of grass blades hitting and rubbing against each other, you're good. If it sounds even vaguely like rain, it will sound more like rain when you get home with no visual cues to guide you otherwise. You may have traveled a long way to get this sound, so work on the illusion until it is just right and evokes the mental image you wish to convey. Keep in mind that lavaliere mics tend to be a bit noisy, but the loud signal of the wind through the blades of grass should mitigate that problem.

The pitched sound of whistling wind is my favorite effect. It is also difficult to find, isolate, and record. The best example I found was by walking a line of a barbed wire fence on a windy spring day in the high plains of Montana, although I'm sure a barbed wire fence in Saskatchewan, Wyoming, South Dakota, or the Pampas of Argentina would do just as well. Set your mics directly on the ground wherever the twists in the taut wire are nearest to the ground and can modulate the pitch; then, begin to record. You might also try an experiment in recording the wind in your own home; when the wind is blowing hard, crack open a window in your house on a particularly windy night and set the mic back a foot or so from the opening. It is not necessary to use lavaliere mics for this one. Nearly any type will do. The effect can be compelling (as long as you live in a relatively quiet neighborhood).

))) **Wind in the Reeds: A Case Study**

On a cold October morning years ago, while working with the Nez Perce Tribe on their Idaho reservation, I was invited by an Elder to visit a sacred tribal spot in northeastern Oregon. He suggested that I sit by the side of a stream and consider the ways in which music might have been revealed to his ancestors. I remained still and heard nothing for a long time. As the late morning wind began to blow down the length of the canyon, I heard what sounded like a giant pipe organ. I had no idea what caused it. Angus Wilson, the Elder, pointed out that certain reeds by the stream's edge had been broken at different lengths; brushed by the force of the wind, the reeds whistled at different pitches. I understood immediately how it was that his ascendants came to create their flute-like instruments and make music inspired by the breath of the forest.

The plains grasslands are home to many bird species, prairie dog colonies, coyotes, and, of course, lots of domestic animals. On any spring and summer day, the sounds of ravens and meadowlarks are featured creatures. You may also hear raptors as well. Before you travel to a place that may be unfamiliar to you, brush up on the area's natural history with a good field guide. Make a "to record" list of some of the animals, insects, and geophonies you hope to hear. These recordings will become elegant souvenirs of your trip to that bioregion.

A few special habitats to explore

Reverberant habitats, such as those created by the *kopjes* (pronounced "copies") in some parts of the southeastern Africa continent and particularly in Zimbabwe, are areas where animals are able to create echoing vocalizations. The kopjes are large granite outcroppings—sometimes as high as 300 feet—that rise out of the flat terrain. During the night, dew settles on the surfaces of the rock and on the scrub vegetation that grows here. The ambient sound of this special environment includes a remarkable reverberant theater in which several species of birds and mammals love to project their voices. On a typical African spring morning, you might hear a troop of baboons bouncing sound off of a nearby kopje; they can modulate their voices in astounding ways. With loud, sharp, bark-like vocalizations, they project sound toward the cliffs, then wait until the echoes of their voices die before performing the same sound all over again. Sometimes they use the reverberation as a duet mechanism where one baboon will bark sharply, followed by another bark so that it can accompany the sound of its own dying echoes. I happened to capture this moment on tape one morning along with the sounds of a rattling cisticola, kurrichane thrush, green-spotted dove, bleating warbler, chinspot battis, buffback shrike, red-billed wood hoopoe, and a bru bru *(CD Track 15).*

Reverberant sound projection can occur in nearly every habitat except deserts. Here are a few examples:

- the pre-dawn voices of hyenas echoing in the forest scrub of the Masai Mara, in Africa
- the cry of wolves around Glacier Bay in Alaska
- killer whales bouncing sound off the cliffs of Johnstone Straight in eastern Vancouver Island
- humpback whales trumpeting off of Pt. Adolphus in Alaska's Icy Strait
- red-tailed hawks on early mornings in northeastern Oregon
- ravens circling high over mountain lakes on early misty mornings in the springtime

Many times, when I've been half awake listening to these ethereal sounds, the creature echoes gave me the eerie dreamlike feeling that what I'm hearing is coming from a source under water.

Insect habitats are among the most surprising sound discoveries. The first time I heard insect larvae in a pool of water by the curb outside my house I was thrilled. I had been experimenting with the hydrophone and decided to drop it into the puddle formed by a spring rainstorm. The small pool of water was alive with sounds that I later realized were caused by water boatmen, a small insect that thrives on decaying wood underwater, and the larvae of insects that I could not immediately identify. It's worth obtaining some special gear to hear such wonders: our ears were meant to hear just fine in air, but not in water. The world of marine sound can be astounding.

In the insect world, ants are among the most extraordinary creatures to record. We cannot hear ants with our unaided ears alone (unless you like the idea of fire ants crawling up your Eustachian tube). However, we certainly can hear some species with the help of small, inexpensive, lavaliere microphones that are laid over the top of the main entrance to the ants' underground home. I defy folks to keep a straight face when they hear the delightful voices of these creatures for the first time. Our ears were meant to hear sounds at some low levels, but are not refined enough to hear the subtlest smaller creatures who do produce sound.

Altered or damaged habitats, such as the one I found at Yuba Pass in California, are important places to explore and record, particularly if you have been able to record the same area prior to when it was damaged. The damage may result from a number of circumstances, not least of which are housing developments, logging, and other signs of "progress." Fire, flood, and other acts of nature, can also alter, transform and damage an area.

In 1988, I visited Lincoln Meadow at the Yuba Pass ridge-line. It is a wide swath of meadowland, usually replete with wildflowers, fledging birds, and a clear trout stream that stretches from the southern end at the edge of the woods diagonally to the northern-most point. Fortunately, I have a record of that moment on tape with all the mystery and magic of the wild soundscape I found intact there. A year later, when I returned, logging had taken place at the southern end of the meadow *(CD Track 8)*. The features that had once made Lincoln Meadow such an enchanted place, were no longer there, and what natural environment that remained was signed as "off-limits" by the lumber company working in the area.

Enough of the primary forest at the southern end had been cleared away, resulting in the runoff of soils that caused the stream to become silty and cloudy as it ran downhill. On this second visit, I recorded the wild soundscape again and documented how it had been incredibly altered. My two recordings provided unique "before and after" samples of how Lincoln Meadow once sounded and how it had changed after logging. When I returned a third time in June 2001, I found that much of the meadow and the stream area had recovered their visual beauty but the dawn chorus of birdsong remained surprisingly meager. Lincoln Meadow was nothing like the vital habitat that had once entranced me and that I had been fortunate enough to capture on tape.

Time to Get Started

We need many, many more before and after examples like this. I encourage you to collect patterns in the natural soundscapes that exist in your area and beyond. Be on the lookout for environments that are destined for some kind of dramatic change, such as areas on the outskirts of a city where future housing tracts may encroach and replace surrounding fields, hill-sides, or wetlands.

Wild soundscapes, biophonies, geophonies and many of the other ideas in this book are concepts that present a new way to relate to the wild natural. The possible habitats you've just read about are only a few among many thousands (at least) that you could explore. Take time to discover the unique wild sounds of some of these locales, or think of ones I haven't mentioned. This is a great way to plan a vacation, an exciting way to go around the world, a way to make the world your home. You have the necessary tools to embark on some of the most joyous experiences of your life. I just wish I could come along to see the look of delight when you put on your headphones and switch on your recorder for the first time.

When the animals come to us,
asking for our help,
will we know what they are saying?

When the plants speak to us
in their delicate, beautiful language,
will we be able to answer them?

When the planet herself
sings to us in our dreams,
will we be able to wake ourselves, and act?

—Gary Lawless

Afterword

We are too content with our sensory extensions, with the fulfillment of

that ice age mind that began its journey amidst the cold of vast tundras

and that pauses only briefly before its leap into space. It is no longer

enough to see as a man sees — even to the ends of the universe.

It is not enough to...see the lightning, or times past, or time to come,

as a man would see it. If we continue to do this, the great brain —

the human brain — will be only a new version of the old trap,

and nature is full of traps for the beast that cannot learn.

—Loren Eiseley

A Fantasy

For one day each spring, the cities, parks, open country and wildlife preserves are filled with nearly the entire population of America, young and old, from the miners underground, teachers in our schools, astronauts in training, to the President and his cabinet. Each willing person is equipped with a mic and sound recorder. The President has decreed this day a holiday called "National Soundscape Day", and on this day there would not be a plane in the sky, a motor vehicle on the ground or a piece of machinery in operation. Everyone would focus on the sounds of non-human creatures and natural phenomena like streams, ocean waves, and wind in trees. In quiet contemplation, people would peacefully work in small groups to record their respective habitats. Those in the cities would record urban birds and the whisper of leaves in a gentle breeze. Those in the country would capture the bird and insect life that populates woodlands, fields, and groves. Others would cover mountain and foothill habitats. Some would record thunderstorms or tornadoes. Still others, inland lakes and the sea shore. Nothing would remain unheard, unlistened-to, unacknowledged on that day of honoring what is divinely provided to us. How else will we be able to hear the howl of the wolf or coyote, or the fragile voices of ants, fish, or a desert tortoise? How else would we be able to hear the lingering message from Eden's garden? Sure. This is a far-fetched dream. Some of the best ideas begin that way.

Nearly a third of the wild habitats I've listened to and recorded since 1968 in North America are either destroyed or seriously altered as of this writing. I feel fortunate for having heard some splendid biophonies during the course of my life. Many now exist only as transformed particles of oxide on an audio tape hidden away on a dark shelf somewhere in my library.

These vital soundscapes have enriched me beyond measure. Natural sounds have engaged my imagination, raising questions about what—and how—we've learned about ourselves in order to be present within wildness. They've lulled me to sleep at night. They've stemmed physical pain and nausea where no other antidote had the slightest effect. They've calmed me in moments of incredible terror and stress. I implore everyone to treasure these miraculous elixirs. Do everything in your power to help preserve what is left and more than anything, listen.

In order to hear natural soundscapes we must actively promote conditions where it becomes possible to do so. Using positive examples from other countries, we need be aware that in 1992, a French law set the limit of 65dBA for environmental sound averaged over a 24-hour period. The World Health Organization has established 55dBA as a desirable daytime limit and 45dBA as a nighttime limit.[1] In the meantime, traffic everywhere is on a colossal upward curve. Perhaps we can match or better the French and WHO numbers through legislation and enforcement. Currently, increased noise comes from many sources: for instance, truck miles traveled in 1995 were 583 percent higher than in 1960, according to Department of Transport statistics; and air miles flown by cargo planes, alone, were up 2,256 percent over 1960 figures.[2] At this rate of increase, masking noise—noise blocking all necessary—in American urban centers will be so loud by 2010 that nothing but mechanical noise will be hearable.

Places of Refuge

Many choose vacations based on traveling into the bosom of the natural world or they listen to recordings in their homes or offices to secure a few moments of serenity. Some of us prefer the ocean and tropical islands.

Others prefer the mountains, the desert, the tall-grass prairies of Montana, or the badlands of the Dakotas. The BaBenzele (Bayaka) Pygmies, living in the Central African Republic, try as often as possible to abandon the urban and rural roads where they've been drawn into the cash economies of European or Japanese loggers. When separated from the forest, they become physically and mentally stressed and overwhelmed—just like us. In order to heal themselves, they know they must return to their ritual deep forest hunts. Louis Sarno, an American living among the Bayaka for nearly two decades, reports that after three months back in the forest most disease-like symptoms disappear.[3] Soundscape is a major component of what leads and holds them there. As their forests are logged and shipped to Europe or Japan, the BaBenzele are saddened and under great pressure. They sense that all the non-human players, with whom they have shared so much, are in danger of losing their homes. They are anxious that they may be losing as well the symphony that they have listened to, performed in, and worshipped for millennia. They are fully aware of what is being lost. The types of sound we gravitate toward comprise our "totem" sounds; they ground or soothe us, make us feel complete, and even spiritually connected.

Listening is but a part of our experience in the wild natural. Because it is the least explored, I have emphasized it here in an effort to bring into balance its awesome presence—an element particularly needed considering our graphic emphasis of the world. Furthermore, I have raised some questions and issues that I hope will be cause for further consideration by new generations of listeners and recordists.

Listening and recording offer us a compelling extension to our limited visual human perspectives. These activities provide us with opportunities to explore our living world, allowing us to better understand and appreciate our place in the web of life. Natural soundscapes are a physical and spiritual elixir. Of course, to incorporate healing sounds—those that calm and center us—into our lives, we must be still, shut our mouths, turn off the incessant noise raging in our heads, along with the televisions, radios, cell phones, automobiles and all the other clamorous noise-generating products that clutter our lives.

A healing magical ingredient is inherent in the simplicity of wild soundscapes—a core frequency that resonates with every living fiber in our bodies. Noise stresses many of us and causes us to become irritable, even volatile. It makes us scream just to heard and noticed above the din; instead, we only need be quiet in order to make a significant mark on the world. The quieter we are on the outside, the more peaceful we become inside. The voices of the natural world are unambiguous on that valuable lesson to us.

Yet these phenomenal biophonies—these concertos of the natural world—are now under serious threat of annihilation. Not only are we moving toward a silent spring, but are quickly advancing toward a silent summer, fall, and winter, as well.

Natural soundscape, being the ancient source and inspiration of our music, dances, and spiritual life, deserve a special place in our hierarchy of high virtues and values. Its many voices taught us the earliest melodies in our human repertoire and inspired major symphonies. Its rhythms have compelled us to take up the flute and the drum and to move our bodies; its unseen sounds conjure visions of spirits hiding deep within the forest. Although this sonorous voice grows dimmer each day, some ancient call spurs us to try and capture every fading utterance. We are too often endowed with a sense of self-importance, and too far removed from recognizing the necessary synaptic link to our own creature roots. These are difficult lessons to learn—especially because we have so much culturally invested in our primacy.

I am particularly drawn to the voices of the wild natural because they deliver a far more substantial and immediate assessment of our current relationship to life on earth than any other factor. These voices tell me that, despite all our destructive claims to power, we are, at best, co-equals. Even recent DNA discoveries confirm that we are not that far removed from what we consider to be the lowly worm. Everywhere, we are in danger of losing our precious extended family. We need to do all we humanly can to cherish and protect the chorus of wild soundscapes. Hopefully, it is not too late to realize that this is the divine message we all need to hear.

1. WHO *Environmental Health Criteria 12*, (Geneva: 1980, p. 19.)

2. Schafer, R. Murray. *The Book of Noise.* (Arcana Editions: Indian River, Ontario, Canada, 1998.)

3. Sarno, L. *Bayaka: The Extraordinary Music of the BaBenzele Pygmies,* book and compact disc recording. (Ellipsis Arts: Roslyn, NY, 1996.)

Binaural Recording Issues

by Lang Elliott

Thanks to field recordist Lang Elliott who offers the following explanation regarding the effect of binaural.

If you record using a binaural-type setup (using two omni mics placed at a comparable distance to the space between your ears and mounted in a head-like holder), then you are theoretically preserving the "spatial cues" that our brains use to determine the whereabouts of sounds in natural situations. These include signal time arrival differences at each ear, intensity differences between ears due to the head-shadowing effect, and phase differences depending on frequency, plus other subtle stuff like head size, shape, and the size and shape of the pinnae.

In order to feed these cues back to the brain on playback, it is critical that a clean left mic signal is channeled to the left ear and a clean right mike signal reaches the right ear. What you don't want is for the left ear to hear the right signal, and vice versa, because such "crosstalk" will cancel out the spatial cues that are so valuable to us when trying to determine the source of a particular sound within a soundscape.

Headphone listening, to some extent, meets these criteria, but has some apparent weaknesses. The main weakness is that, due to the physical closeness of the headphones, speaker elements to the ears, many of the resulting sounds appear to come from within one's head, rather than "out in a spatial soundscape" where they belong. This is especially a problem with sounds originating front and center; these sounds appear largely to be "in one's head" when using headphones, even when the recording was made using a high quality binaural miking technique.

Conventional "stereo" speaker playback completely destroys spatial cues because of crosstalk (= because our right ear hears the left speaker and our left ear hears right speaker). Thus, even if the recording is rich in spatial cues, they are degraded by the stereo playback technique itself. The result is that we end up having to rely on a very unnatural way to determine the whereabouts of sound sources, based primarily on intensity differences between the two speakers. A sound that is louder in the right speaker will appear to come from that direction, and vice versa. Sounds appear to come from the center when they are of equal loudness in both speakers. This explains the familiar "phantom center" in stereo playback. Conventional stereo is a system full of acoustic compromises that tends to compress and distort spaciousness and localization, though it admittedly sounds good if one has never heard a better alternative. It is what we're used to.

One can reduce or eliminate the crosstalk problem in several ways. An easy, but awkward solution is to use a barrier. It goes like this: set two speakers together and insert a barrier between them, such as a 3 feet tall by 4 feet long piece of plywood extending out toward the listener. Then, sit at the end of the barrier, with your nose to the barrier, and listen to a binaural nature recording. Suddenly, you will hear sounds extending out in an arc approaching 150 degrees, far wider than a stereo soundstage, and incredibly dimensional and realistic. It is called 3-D sound because of the marvelous sense of depth. It is referred to as "Virtual" 3-D because sounds aren't really coming from where you hear them. What's happening is that our brains are receiving the natural spatial cues in the binaural recording and thus our brains automatically place the sounds where they're supposed to be.

Now there are "crosstalk canceling" solutions that allow a listener to remove the barrier and still get the same effect, as long as the listener sits along the axis between the speakers at an optimal distance. One such system, the UltraQ, accomplishes this using proprietary analog circuitry. Other more advanced solutions involve DSP processing that will enable to pre-process recordings before playing them back and, perhaps, even encoding the binaural signal with the anti-crosstalk format.

Some crosstalk-canceling solutions work best with the speakers placed apart, either at the conventional 60 degree equilateral triangle position (meaning that the listener forms the apex of an equilateral triangle with speakers located in front), or else with the speakers a little closer together. A couple of the more recent and advanced DSP solutions work optimally if the speakers are place much closer together, at a 15-20 degree angle with respect to the listener.

Some Terms Used in this Book

*This glossary includes the terms contained in this book that were printed in **bold italic type**, as well as additional terms and expressions used in the field of bio-acoustics.*

acoustic - pertaining to the physics of sound.

acoustic boundaries - refers to an amoeba-shaped boundary within which particular creatures vocalize (as part of mating, feeding, conflict, etc.); a territory defined by its sound signatures.

acoustic ecology - the study of how sound in given environments affects humans and non-humans, alike; a term brought into the lexicon by R. Murray Schafer in the late 1970s.

acoustic signature - a characteristic sound pattern, call, or vocalization that belongs to any species or unique member of that species.

acoustic texture - the quality or dimensionality of particular sounds or bio-phonies.

ambient - surrounding, encircling, as in sounds that seem to permeate and envelope a biome or mini-biome.

amplifier - a device designed to control audio levels.

amplitude - signal level measured in decibels.

audio spectrum - the range of sounds, from lowest to highest, one can hear.

bioacoustician - one who studies the sounds of living organisms.

bioacoustics - the sounds of living organisms.

binaural - sound transmission emanating from two sources which may vary acoustically, as in tone or pitch, to give a stereophonic effect.

biome - a large, naturally occurring community of flora and fauna occupying a major habitat, such as a forest, grassland, or tundra; a region or biotic community, characterized by particular forms of life that occupy the region.

biophony - creature symphony; the whole soundscape of a habitat or specific biome.

cacophony - a din of noise created by unrelated sound.

cans - slang or jargon for headphones.

cardioid - heart shaped microphone pick-up pattern.

collective sound - a biophony, or whole sound resulting from an animal community.

contact vocalizations - sounds made by creatures in order to identify, warn, or otherwise communicate with one another (within their own species, generally).

DAT - Digital Audio Tape.

decibel (dB) - the common practical unit for the logarithmic expression for ratios of loudness, power, voltage, current, etc.; one unit of change relates to the smallest shift that the human ear can detect.

distortion - occurs when the normal shape of the audio wave form is altered in a manner so that it no longer conveys the information cohesively. (In professional terms, this occurs when the amplitude of a signal exceeds the ability of the technology to read or record it. That occurrence is referred to as *clipping*. Another type of distortion introduced by the inability of digital equipment to read very high frequency signals is called *aliasing*. And yet another is introduced by the inability of a microphone to read and capture certain complex signals that contain unrelated harmonic content.)

echo - the discernible repetition of reflected sound waves in both indoor and outdoor habitats.

echolation - the location of objects by reflected sound, in particular as used by animals such as bats or dolphins. Also called *echolocation*.

ecotone - a transitional zone between one type of biome, or area typified by certain life forms, and another.

equalizer – a device that can increase signal strength in selected portions of the audible spectrum in a recording.

field (as in near field, mid-field, and far field) - the audible scope or range of sound as received by the ear or a transducer.

filter - a device for attenuating selected portions of the audible spectrum.

frequency - the number of complete cycles of a periodic signal occurring in a given time span. The unit in general use is designated in terms of Hertz (Hz) and where 1Hz. is equal to one cycle per second.

geophony - non-human natural sounds such as streams, wind in the trees, thunder, rain, earthquakes, avalanches.

habitat - the natural home or environment of an organism.

Hertz (Hz.) - a unit of frequency in the field of acoustics defined as one cycle per second (see *frequency*).

hydrophone - an underwater microphone.

infrasound - usually referred to as those sounds lower in frequency (less than 20Hz) than the human capacity to detect.

kopje - (also *koppie*) a jumbled granite outcropping found in Africa; the term derives from Dutch, *kop*, diminutive for "head."

lek - a patch of ground used for communal display in the breeding season by the males of certain birds and mammals, especially black grouse (kind of like a singles bar).

loudness - refers to the perceived intensity of sound. Loudness is not always a measure of sound pressure level and can be sensed as being loud by virtue of its particular texture or timbre.

M-S - a two channel microphone system consisting of two different types of mics, one being a type of cardioid pattern, and the second, a figure eight pattern. (The resultant recording provides numerous options for archiving and mixing. An M-S decoder is required to transform a M-S recording into a conventional left/right stereo image.)

mangrove - a shrubby tree that grows in muddy, chiefly tropical, coastal swamps and has tangled roots that grow above ground forming dense thickets.

microphone - a device that transforms vibrations transmitted through the air into corresponding electrical signals.

mic - slang for microphone.

MD - mini-disc.

mix – any choice an artist makes with regard to what remains in the final expression of a recording.

monaural – a single channel recording designed for listening with one ear.

monophonic – a class of recorded sound originating from a single media track.

noise - for the purpose of this document, unwanted sound; any sound that impairs accurate transmission of useful and helpful information.

noise-free intervals - 15 minute periods when there is no mechanical or domestic noise presence.

noise pollution - a relatively recent concept that an environment can be impacted and harmed by the intrusion of unwanted sound.

noise shadow - absence of noise.

octave - a difference in frequency (Hz.) of either double or half in relation to a primary tone. In a Western, diatonic music scale, an octave is the eighth tone in the musical scale higher or lower from a fundamental pitch.

optical sound track - a method of producing sound on film by a type of narrow bar-code-like stripe running along one side of the film strip. A beam of light is projected onto, and through, the stripe as it moves through the film projector sprockets. The beam, modulated by the dark and light patterns of the stripe, is picked up by a light-sensing photoelectric cell that translates the patterns into sound.

overtone - a tone that is part of a harmonic series but which is higher than the fundamental note, and may be heard with it.

parabolic dish - a bowl-shaped apparatus designed to focus and capture sound from a distance.

pitch - often perceived as frequency but more subjective since it is dependent on both the loudness and timbre of the sound produced.

quiet - absence of noise but sometimes the inclusion of desired sound.

quietude - a state of quiet and calm.

reverberation - repetitions of sound that are so closely spaced in time as not to be individually discernible. These phenomena occur in both indoor and outdoor environments.

reverberant habitats - an environment that, due to its unique geographical features, allows for the reverberation of animal and other sounds, such as the *kopjes* in Africa.

riparian - of, or relating to, or situated on the banks of a river.

sample - to take all or parts of a sound out of its original context so that it can be placed in another context. The term also includes the method of recording a sound into a musical instrument sampler in order to play it back with different pitches or durations.

sensory niche - the whole sensory environment that an animal experiences in its habitat.

shock-mount - a mic mounting system designed to attenuate shock waves.

signal-to-noise - in recording, this is the ratio of "useful information" or signal (i. e., what is desirable to record) to unwanted noise (i. e., noise produced by record electronics, or other background sound). If the signal is loud enough in relation to the noise, the noise will tend to be imperceptible.

sonogram - see spectrogram

sound mirror - the forerunner of the parabolic dish, a device used to capture sound originating a considerable distance from the microphone.

sound safari - a trip, adventure or exploration with the focus on listening to and recording wild soundscapes or biophonies.

soundscape - the entire acoustic environment of our lives.

sound sculpture - taking sound, the medium with which we work, and sculpting it much as artists in any "hard" form (clay, metal, ceramic, etc.) do.

The results, when commissioned to the fullest extent of technical and production capabilities, are three-dimensional audio performances that fill anything from small spaces to whole large rooms.

sound signature - the unique quality of a sound.

sound wave - a unit of acoustic energy.

spectrogram - (also called *sonogram* or *voice print*) a visual representation of sound featuring time on one axis, frequency on another, and amplitude by light or dark gray scale of the image.

spectrum - in audio, the ability of a device (ear, microphone, recorder, etc.) to detect or reproduce sound. (Humans have the ability to hear a frequency anywhere between 20Hz and 20kHz., which is typically cited as the normal range of reproducible sound in most professional and semi-professional recording gear.)

stereo - a class of recorded sounds that typically begins with two microphones (or one system with two mic elements) set in relationship to one another so that spatial information of the environment is captured, or at least the resulting recording creates the illusion that this is so. (For the purposes of this document, it includes XY, MS, and binaural recording.)

streaming audio - a digital format for transmitting an audio signal over the web.

stridulation - friction between body parts causing a sound.

territorial syntax - (see *sound signature*)

timbre - the unique quality of a given voice or combination of voices which can signify the character of a particular bird, mammal or amphibian, instrument in a human orchestra, or combinations of instruments or creature voices (see *biophony*). (Sometimes this sound characteristic is referred to as *tone color*.)

tone - usually referred to as a constant frequency or pitch.

transducer - in recording, any device that either receives or transmits audio signals by converting one type of energy into another. These include microphones, headphones, and audio speakers.

ultrasound - usually referred to as those sounds higher in frequency (more than 20kHz) than the human capacity to detect.

voice print - (see *spectrogram*).

XY - a form of stereo using two directional mics set in specific relationship to each other.

wild natural - a term used instead of nature to describe the collective voice of creatures, the creatures individually, and their habitats.

windscreen - wind protector for microphones.

Reading and Resources

Reading

Abbey, Edward. *Down the River*. (New York, NY: E. P. Dutton, 1982.)

Abram, David. *The Spell of the Sensuous*. (New York, NY: Pantheon, 1996.)

Berendt, Joachim-Ernst. *The Third Ear*. (New York, NY: Owl Books, Henry Holt & Co., 1992.)

Carson, Rachael. *Silent Spring*. (Boston, MA: Houghton Mifflin Co., 1962.)

Chatwin, Bruce. *Songlines*. (New York, NY: Penguin Books, 1987.)

Eiseley, Loren. *The Night Country*. (New York, NY: Scribners, 1971.)

_____ *The Unexpected Universe*. (New York, NY: Harcourt Brace, 1994.)

Feld, Steven. *Sound and Sentiment: Birds, Weeping, Poetics and Song in Kaluli Expression*. (Philadelphia, PA: University of Pennsylvania Press, 1990.)

Krause, B. L. *Notes from the Wild* (with CD). (Roslyn, NY: Ellipsis Arts, 1996.)

_____ *Into a Wild Sanctuary*. (Berkeley, CA: Heyday Books, 1998.)

Lyon, Thomas. *Noise and the Sacred*. (Salt Lake City, UT: Utah Wilderness Association Review, May/June 1995.)

Mathieu, W.A. *The Listening Book: Discovering Your Own Music*. (Boston, MA: Shambala Press, 1991.

_____ *A Musical Life*. (Boston, MA: Shambala Press, 1994.)

Sarno, Louis. *The Extraordinary Music of the BaBenzele Pygmies*. (book and CD), (Roslyn, NY: Ellipsis Arts, 1996.)

Schafer, R. Murray. *Tuning of the World* (in the United States under the title: *Soundscape*). (New York, NY: Knopf 1977.)

_____ *Voices of Tyranny: Temples of Silence*. (Indian River, Ontario: Arcana Editions, 1993.)

_____ *The Book of Noise*. (Indian River, Ontario: Arcana Editions, 1998.)

Shepard, Paul. *The Others: How Animals Made Us Human*. (Washington, DC: Island Press, 1996.)

_____ *Nature & Madness*. (San Francisco, CA: Sierra Club Books, 1982.)

Streicher, R. and Everest, F. Alton. *The New Stereo Review, 2nd Edition.* (Pasadena, CA: Audio Engineering Associates, 1998.)

Wilson, E. O. *Biodiversity.* (Washington, DC: National Academy Press, 1988.)

Some Recommended Guide Books

Borror, D.J. *Field Guide to Insects—America North of Mexico.* (Boston, MA: Houghton Mifflin, 1998.)

Cogger, H.G. *Encyclopedia of Reptiles and Amphibians.* (New York, NY: Academic Press, 1998.)

Elliott, Lang. *Music of the Birds: A Celebration of Bird Song* (book and CD). (Boston, MA: Houghton Mifflin Press, 1999.)

Lieske, E., and Myers, R. *Coral Reef Fishes.* (Princetown, NJ: Princeton University Press, 1996.)

Milne, L.J. *National Audubon Society Field Guide to North American Insects and Spiders.* (New York, NY: Knopf, 1980.)

Mound, L. *Eyewitness: Insect.* (London/New York, NY: DK Publishing, 2000.)

Paxton, J.R. *Encyclopedia of Fishes, 2nd Edition.* (New York, NY: Academic Press, 1998.)

Resources

Organizations

British Library of Wildlife Sounds.
http://www.bl.uk/collections/soundarchive/wild.html

Cornell University, Library of Natural Sounds. **http://birds.cornell.edu/LNS/**

NatureRecordists. **naturerecordists@yahoogroups.com**
An informational chat format for field recording and technology at all levels of interest.

Nature Sounds Society. Oakland Museum. 1000 Oak St., Oakland, CA 94607, **http://www.naturesounds.org**
Programs and introductory field workshops.

Noise Pollution Clearinghouse. Les Blomberg, P. O. Box 1137, Montpelier, VT 05601-1137, Tel.:1-888-200-8332, **http://www.nonoise.org**

Quiet Down America. **http://www.quietdownamerica.com**

Wild Sanctuary. **http://www.wildsanctuary.com**

World Forum for Acoustic Ecology.
http://interact.uoregon.edu/MediaLit/WFAEHomePage

Soundscape Outfitters and Guides

Spirit Walker Expeditions, Gustavus, Alaska, 1-800-529-2537
   www.seakayakalaska.com
   Specializing in SE Alaska.

On Safari International, Harare, Zimbabwe
   osi@ecoweb.co.zw or **solomon@mweb.co.zw** (Derek Solomon)
   Specializing in south, south-central, and east Africa sound safaris.

Discography

Bernie Krause

A Wild Christmas (w/ Phil Aaberg)	Wild Sanctuary 1998
African Adventures	Wild Sanctuary 1998
All Good Men (w/ Paul Beaver)	Warner Brothers 1973
Alpine Meadow	Wild Sanctuary 2002
Amazon Days, Amazon Nights	Wild Sanctuary 1998
Borneo: Paradise in Kalimantan	Wild Sanctuary 1998
Citadels of Mystery	Takoma/Mobile Fidelity 1979
Dawn at Trout Lake	Wild Sanctuary 1998
Desert Solitudes (w/ Ruth Happel)	Wild Sanctuary 1994
Discover the Wonder (Grades 3–6)	Scott Foresman 1992
Distant Thunder	Nature Company 1988
Equator	Nature Company 1986
Gandharva (w/ Paul Beaver)	Warner Brothers 1971
Gentle Ocean	Nature Company 1988
Gorilla	Nature Company 1989
Gorillas in the Mix	Rykodisk 1989
Green Meadow Stream	Wild Sanctuary 1998
In a Wild Sanctuary (w/ Paul Beaver)	Warner Brothers 1969
Ishi, the Last Yahi	Wild Sanctuary 1992
Jungle Shoes/Fish Wrap	Rykodisk 1988
Mata Atlantica (Atlantic Rainforest, w/ R. Happel)	
	Wild Sanctuary 1994
Meridian (w/ Phil Aaberg)	Nature Company 1990
Midsummer Nights (w/ Ruth Happel)	Wild Sanctuary 1998
Morning Song Birds	Nature Company 1988
Mountain Stream	Nature Company 1988

Music of the Nez Perce	Wild Sanctuary 1991
Natural Voices/African Song Cycle	Wild Sanctuary 1990
Nature	Nature Company 1987
Nature's Lullabies (Wee Creatures Ages 1-3): Ocean, Rain & Stream (3 titles)	Wild Sanctuary 1994
Nez Perce Stories	Wild Sanctuary 1991
Nonesuch Guide to Electronic Music	Nonesuch 1968
Ocean Dreams	Wild Sanctuary 1998
Ocean Odyssey (w/ Rodney Franklin)	Wild Sanctuary 1998
Ocean Wonders	Wild Sanctuary 1998
Ragnarok (w/ Paul Beaver)	Limelite 1969
Rainforest Dreams (w/ Rodney Franklin)	Wild Sanctuary 1998
Revised Nonesuch Guide to Electronic Music	Nonesuch 1979
Rhythms of Africa (w/ Rodney Franklin)	Wild Sanctuary 1998
Sounds of a Summer's Evening	Nature Company 1988
Tropical Rainforest	Nature Company 1989
Tropical Thunder	Wild Sanctuary 1991
Tundra in Spring	Wild Sanctuary 2002
Whales, Wolves & Eagles of Glacier Bay	Wild Sanctuary 1998
Wild Times at the Waterhole	Wild Sanctuary 1991
Woodland Journey	Wild Sanctuary 1990

Others

Antarctica (Doug Quin)*	Wild Sanctuary 1998
*Bayaka: The Extraordinary Music of the BaBenzele Pygmies** (Louis Sarno)	Ellipsis Arts 1996
Drums Across the Tundra (Chuna McIntyre)	Wild Sanctuary 1992
*Loons of Echo Pond** (Ruth Happel)	Wild Sanctuary 1998
Madagascar: Gardens of Eden (Doug Quin)*	Wild Sanctuary 1998

**Bernie Krause, Executive Producer

The Poems in this Book

Grateful acknowledgment is extended to the following writers and publishers for allowing us to quote from their work:

p. 11   Hermann Hesse. "Sometimes," from *News from the Universe: Poems of Twofold Consciousness*, Robert Bly, translator and ed. (Sierra Club Books: San Francisco, CA, 1980.) Reprinted in *Earth Prayers From Around the World*, Elizabeth Roberts and Elias Amidon, eds. (HarperSanFrancisco, a division of HarperCollins Publishers: New York, NY, 1991.)

p. 43   Gabon Pygmy, Africa. "All Lives, All Dances, & All is Loud," from *Technicians of the Sacred: A Range of Poetries from Africa, America, Asia, Europe & Oceania*, 2nd edition, Jerome Rothenberg, ed. (University of California Press: Berkeley, CA, 1968, 1985.) Permission graciously given by Jerome Rothenberg.

p. 47   José Emilio Pacheco. "Defense and Illustration of Poetry," from *An Ark for the Next Millennium: Poems by José Emilio Pacheco*, translations by Margaret Sayers Peden; selections by Jorge Esquinca. (The University of Texas Press: Austin, TX, 1993.)

p. 50   Marcia Falk. "Listen," from *The Book of Blessings*. (HarperSanFrancisco, 1996; paperback edition, Beacon Press, 1999.) Copyright © 1996 by Marcia Lee Falk. Used by permission of the author.

p. 51   Orpingalik, a Netsilik Eskimo. A statement from *Technicians of the Sacred*, cited above.

p. 98   Gwendolyn B. Bennett. "Quatrain 2," from *Shadowed Dreams: Women's Poetry of the Harlem Renaissance*, Maureen Honey, ed. (Rutgers University Press: New Brunswick, CT, 1989.)

p. 122   Aboriginal from Arnhem Land, Australia. A poem from *Technicians of the Sacred*, cited above.

p. 124   William Butler Yeats. "The Lake Isle of Innisfree," from *The Yeats Reader*, Richard J. Finneran, ed. (Scribner Poetry: New York, NY, © 1997 by Anne Yeats.)

p. 144   Lawless, Gary. "When the Animals Come to Us," from *Earth Prayers From Around the World*, cited above. First published in *First Sight of Land*. (Blackberry Books: Nobelboro, MN.) Permission graciously given by the author.

Animal Illustrations in this Book

The images of animals used in this book were derived from:

Animals: 1419 Copyright-Free Illustrations of Mammals, Birds, Fish, Insects, etc., *A Pictorial Archive from Nineteenth-Century Sources*, Jim Harter, ed. (Dover Publications, Inc.: Mineola, NY, 1979.)

cover, clockwise from top right:
>   Siberian songbird, coyote, unidentified insect, European frog

p. iv   European frog

p. xiv   California quail

p. xvi   long-eared bat

p. 12   gazelle

p. 18   wolf

p. 21   salmon *(continued on p. 22)*

p. 23   spotted hyena

p. 39   sea anemone

p. 42   elephant and barnacles

p. 44   bat-eared fox

p. 46   cricket

p. 48   bullfrogs

p. 52   robin

p. 60   song thrush

p. 68   jaguar

p. 96   ants

p. 97   triggerfish

p. 98   water-scavanger beetle

p. 100   coyote

p. 118   wolf

p. 124   honey-bee

p. 126   horned owl

p. 129   jaguar *(tail)*

p. 130   tamarin monkey

p. 134   gorilla

p. 137   fruit bat

p. 138   red deer *(standing in for an elk)*

p. 140   grasses

p. 144   cicada

p. 148   European frog *(again)*

About Wild Sanctuary

Wild Sanctuary is known internationally for natural soundscape recordings and for audio media design in public spaces such as museums, aquaria, zoos, and other large public environments, highlighting rare or extinct habitats throughout the world. You can contact Wild Sanctuary at:

chirp@wildsanctuary.com

or by writing to:

Wild Sanctuary
P. O. Box 536
Glen Ellen, CA 95442
(707) 996-6677

www.wildsanctuary.com

If you have comments, corrections or suggestions about this book that you would like to share with us, please send them to:

Managing Editor
Wilderness Press
1200 5th Street
Berkeley, CA 94710

mail@wildernesspress.com

Index